31
Days of
Praise

Other books by Warren and Ruth Myers

31 Days of Praise
Book and Journal Combination

31 Days of Prayer
Book and Journal Combination
This book will lift you to new heights of prayer and
into a new awareness of God's presence.

Days of Praise

E n j o y i n g
G o d
A n e w

Ruth Myers

with

Warren Myers

Multnomah® Publishers *Sisters, Oregon*

31 DAYS OF PRAISE
published by Multnomah Publishers, Inc.

© 1994 by Warren and Ruth Myers
International Standard Book Number: 1-57673-875-2

Cover image by Photodisc

Unless otherwise indicated, Scripture quotations are from:
New American Standard Bible ©1960, 1977 by the Lockman Foundation

Other Scripture quotations:
The Holy Bible, New International Version (NIV) © 1973, 1984 by International Bible Society, used by permission of Zondervan Publishing House *The Holy Bible,* New King James Version (NKJV) © 1984 by Thomas Nelson, Inc. *The Holy Bible,* King James Version (KJV) *The New Testament in Modern English, Revised Edition* (Phillips) © 1958, 1960, 1972 by J. B. Phillips *The Living Bible* (TLB) © 1971. Used by permission of Tyndale House Publishers, Inc. All rights reserved. *Revised Standard Version Bible* (RSV) © 1946, 1952 by the Division of Christian Education of the National Council of the Churches of Christ in the United States of America *The Inspired Letters in Clearest English,* by Frank C. Laubach (Laubach) © 1956 by Thomas Nelson and Sons *The New Testament: A Translation in the Language of the People* by Charles B. Williams (Williams) ©1937 by Bruce Humphries, Inc., copyright renewed 1965 by Edith S. Williams, Moody Bible Institute

Multnomah is a trademark of Multnomah Publishers, Inc.,
and is registered in the U.S. Patent and Trademark Office.
The colophon is a trademark of Multnomah Publishers, Inc.

Printed in the United States of America

Library of Congress Cataloging-in-Publication Data:
Myers, Warren and Ruth.
31 days of praise / by Warren and Ruth Myers.
    p.   cm.
ISBN 1-57673-334-3
ISBN 1-57673-875-2
1. Praise of God—Prayer-books and devotions—English.
2. Devotional calendars.
I. Title. II. Title: Thirty-one days of praise
BV4817.M93 1994
242'.72—dc20   94-9575
                                           CIP

02 03 04 05 06 07 08—35 34 33 32 31 30

Contents

PART I

PART II

PART III

PART IV

FOREWORD

Thirty-one Days of Praise is down to earth. It touches you where you live and walks with you where you plod. It is not a book that tells you to praise because "you are supposed to" and "you will be blessed" if you do. Rather, it inspires and motivates you to praise from the heart.

This book deals with the realities of living in a fallen world with its disappointing relationships, unfulfilled longings, and shattered dreams. It meets you where you are in the midst of your pain and turmoil and enables you to see these things from a perspective that is true. As a result, even in the face of heartache, there is praise and the joy of a deeper intimacy with God. Praise itself becomes a blessing because it is real, and not just a rehearsal of words.

If you are like some of us, you struggle more with your own sin and failure than with outward circumstances. You may be under too heavy a cloud of unworthiness to think of praise. You may feel that until your life is straightened out you are in no condition to praise.

But *31 Days of Praise* cuts through that darkness and despair with the truth, reminding you that approach to God has nothing to do with your attainment; it is based on Christ's atonement alone. This book will lift your eyes so that you see the purity, honor, and dignity that God has given you, His "beloved" one. That right view of yourself is not only immensely freeing...it also brings both joy and deep praise.

As a teacher, conference speaker, and former dean of women at Multnomah Bible College, I have had the opportunity to review many excellent books over the years. Yet *31 Days of Praise* is the only one that has inspired me to state at my conferences: "Forget buying my books; *this* is a book you must get." In the last year I have seen easily over one thousand copies purchased at my seminars.

The reason for my enthusiasm is easy to explain: *31 Days of Praise* connects with the deep wellsprings of the heart. It brings healing. It releases praise. I have seen it change the lives of many across this country, and other countries as well.

So immerse yourself in *31 Days of Praise.* If you don't know how to begin to praise, it will open up the path for you. If you have trouble verbalizing your feelings, it will help you put into words what is on your heart.

As you use it day by day you'll learn fresh and exciting ways to bring glory and pleasure to God. You'll discover anew your Father's understanding, His deep and abiding compassion for you...the strength of His Word to meet your deepest longings and needs. And above all, you'll experience the boundless joy of giving God the praise that is His due.

Dr. Pamela Reeve
Adviser and professor at
Multnomah Bible College

SPECIAL THANKS AND A BIT OF HISTORY

W arren and I have been amazed by—and very grateful for—the thirty-year process God has used to develop this book.

The story began in the 1960s when I wrote Personal Praise Pages, a mimeographed twenty-day reminder of things to praise the Lord for. In the early seventies I was giving a lecture series at the American Club in Singapore and searching for a tool to help women move toward positive emotions. The praise material came to mind, and I expanded it to include a full month of daily praises. Through the years, Warren and I had heard from people who had obtained copies and were using the praise material in this embryonic form.

The praise pages found their way into the

hands of Gene Warr, a godly businessman from Oklahoma City. His wife, Irma, had used the days of praise for twenty years. Gene began to press us to publish the material in book form. He finally prevailed in 1991, helping out financially and reserving the first seven hundred copies to send as Christmas gifts.

Warren's executive assistant in Singapore, Lim Meng Lee, used her creative resources to help produce and promote the book and within three years more than twenty thousand copies of the first edition were distributed.

In 1994, Warren and I worked together revising, polishing, and amplifying the book for Multnomah Publishers.

The credit for this book goes to many people, but most of all we're grateful to the Lord who in His sovereign grace has chosen to richly use it in many lives.

Ruth Myers

An Invitation
to Praise

If you're just beginning to praise and worship, you're on the threshold of a great adventure. You'll find that your gracious, mighty, and majestic God is delightful beyond imagining. You'll discover what a high privilege it is to praise Him! And whether you're a beginner or someone who has long understood the benefits of praise, you'll find that the more you glorify the Lord, the more He will refresh you and deepen your experience of Him.

This book has been in the making for years. It was born during my years as a widow. It flowed out of truths that had long motivated me to trust and worship the Lord in the varied seasons and experiences of my life—as a single girl in my native land...as a young wife sojourning in Taiwan, in the Philippines, and in Hong Kong...during my first husband's months of intense suffering with cancer before the Lord called him Home...during my years as a widow with two young children.

Woven into this book you'll find truths about God that affirm A. W. Tozer's words: "The man who has God as his treasure has all things in one, and he has it purely, legitimately, and forever."[1]

And you'll find truths that time and again have brought me up short, enabling me to let God into the experiences of my life, whether joyful or painful. Truths that confirm Hudson Taylor's reflections on John 7:37, written about the time his first wife, Maria, died:

"If any man thirst, let him come unto Me and drink."

Who does not thirst? Who has not mind-thirsts or heart-thirsts, soul-thirsts or body-thirsts? Well, no matter which, or whether I have them all—"Come unto Me and" remain thirsty? Ah, no! "Come unto Me and *drink.*"

What, can Jesus meet my need? Yes, and more than meet it. No matter how

intricate my path, how difficult my service;
no matter how sad my bereavement, how
far away my loved ones; no matter how
helpless I am, how deep are my soul
yearnings—Jesus can meet all.
All, and more than meet.[2]

I discovered this in a new way after my first
husband died at the age of thirty-two. I grieved and
shed my tears; I felt deep loneliness, along with the
pressures of being left alone to raise two young
children. At times I felt overwhelmed at making all
the family decisions.

Yet at the same time I found bright rays of
sunlight shining into my heart. How grateful I was to
the Lord for His many blessings: for Brian and Doreen
and the joys of being their mother, for other people in
my life and their loving help, for special answers to
prayer, and for small delights, such as gazing at a sunset
or a unique branch silhouetted against the sky.

And even more, the Lord blessed me through
times of worship and praise, often with tears of joy
mingled with sadness.

I found immense comfort as I expressed to the Lord my grief at losing my loved one, and then let Him speak words of love to my heart. Words like the first part of Isaiah 43:4: "You are precious in my eyes, and honored, and I love you" (RSV). Then I'd tell Him how glad I was that I still had my Most Beloved One with me: "Thank You, Lord, that I can enjoy Your love—the best love of all! Your love is intensely personal; it never fails. And with You I can enjoy an intimacy far beyond what even the dearest earthly loved one could ever offer, for You live in me and You're with me every moment, day and night." As my human aloneness pressed me to love and adore the Lord in new ways, He gave me joy in the midst of sorrow.

As C. H. Spurgeon wrote, our griefs cannot mar the melody of our praise; they are simply the bass notes of our life song: "To God Be the Glory."

The months passed, then the years—eight in all before the Lord brought Warren and me together. And it seemed that God used sorrow and loneliness and perplexities to stretch out spaces in my heart for deeper joy than I'd known before—especially the joy of loving and praising Him.

I discovered that God had also used difficulties to stretch out spaces in Warren's heart for a deeper experience of God and richer prayer and praise. Here is how Warren describes it:

I came to know the Lord in 1945 when I was a pilot in the Air Corps. As He began to draw me closer to Himself, He placed in my heart a hunger for His Word and a deep desire to know Him better. This led me to extended times of prayer and praise and enjoying Him.

During the following year, He worked in my heart, making me willing to install Him as Lord of my life—especially of my future vocation and marriage. My commitment went something like this: "Lord, I put You in total charge of my future—any place, any time, with or without anyone or anything."

This commitment brought scores of delightful benefits. It also led to times of doubt and struggle, especially in the matter of finding a life partner. In a variety

of ways, the Lord closed doors to a
number of bright possibilities. Eventually I
became very interested in a lovely widow
and approached her about the possibility
of beginning a courtship. Ruth's response
was enthusiastic—seven years later!

I was twenty-three when I made
Christ Lord, yielding my future and
marriage to Him. I was forty-six when
Ruth and I were married. What a joy it
has been to live and labor and pray and
praise together for almost thirty years.

It was a deepening experience for Warren and
me to work together on the final writing of *31 Days of
Praise*. We enjoy using the praise pages, both together
and in our personal praise and prayer times.

We're amazed and delighted to see the Lord
using this book in the lives of many men, women,
and young people—in their darkest times as well as
in their best and in-between times. Again and again
people write to tell us how God has used various
days of praise to turn their distresses and struggles
into blessings. We pray He will do the same for you.

OUR GOAL: A LIFESTYLE OF PRAISE

The thirty-one days of praise in this booklet have been designed to help you praise and give thanks both in your times of blessing and in your times of trial. These praise pages will expand your praise life and help you develop the practice of "giving thanks always for all things" (Ephesians 5:20, NKJV). They will help you cultivate a lifestyle of praise.

But before you begin, let's take a look at what praise is and why it's so important—why it's more than a pleasant pastime.

WORSHIP? PRAISE? OR THANKSGIVING?

In the Bible, praise is closely linked with worship and thanksgiving. Through all three we honor and enjoy God.

It helps me to think of worship as a beautiful crown adorned with two brilliant jewels. One jewel is praise; the other, thanksgiving.

Throughout the Bible people expressed their worship in several ways. They bowed before God, often with a sense of awe, to honor Him and show their devotion. They offered special gifts to Him, the chief gift being themselves.

Today, as in Bible times, worship includes yielding to God as our Lord and Master. We see this in Romans 12:1, where God asks us to offer Him our bodies, our lives, our entire person. This, He says, is true worship.

In genuine spiritual worship, we bow before the Most High God, the most merciful and reliable and winsome of all beings, and we crown Him as Lord of all that we are. We consent to His gracious, transforming work in our lives; we agree that He can work in us so that we'll be willing and able to do His will. In other words, we choose to let Him be God in our lives. This is our greatest privilege, the highest thing we can do.

Worship also includes adoring God, admiring Him, appreciating Him, and letting Him know how grateful we are for His mighty works and the blessings He bestows on us. Thus worship includes praise and thanksgiving. As in ancient times, all three—worship, praise, and thanksgiving—overlap as we glorify and enjoy God. Sometimes we do this in speaking, sometimes in singing, sometimes in silent reverence.

In thanksgiving we express gratitude to the Lord for His love and goodness to us and to others, for His constant acts of care, and for His gifts, including the spiritual blessings He has lavished upon us.

In praise we admire God for who He is and what He does. Praise can be quiet and meditative. But it can also include celebrating and exulting in the Lord's majesty and splendor, His sovereignty, His limitless power, and His bountiful love—which we do not in the least deserve. In praise we extol our wonderful God; we exalt and magnify Him. Praise includes speaking highly of God to other people, as well as directly to Him.

So mounted in the crown of worship—the basic act of offering God our lives, of honoring Him as God—are the jewels of praise and thanksgiving. Jewels that radiate the glory of God, to His delight and ours.

It's fine if we blend worship, praise, and thanksgiving any way we like. God isn't in the least concerned if we say "Thank You" when "I praise You" or "I worship You" might be more appropriate. And it doesn't matter whether our words are stumbling or eloquent. God looks on the heart; He's searching for people who simply want to honor Him.

I find that my worship is richer when I offer the Lord praise and thanks for three things: *who He is, what He does,* and *what He gives.*

Over and over the Scriptures encourage us to worship and praise and give thanks.

> By him [Jesus] therefore let us offer the sacrifice of praise to God continually, that is, the fruit of our lips giving thanks to His name. (Hebrews 13:15, KJV)

> Be filled with the Spirit...singing and making melody in your heart to the Lord; Giving thanks always for all things unto God and the Father in the name of our Lord Jesus Christ. (Ephesians 5:18–20, KJV)

These verses remind me of the words of David in Psalm 34: "I will bless the Lord at all times; His praise shall continually be in my mouth." And the aging man in Psalm 71 wrote, "My mouth is filled with your praise, declaring your splendor all day long.... I will praise you more and more" (NIV).

We too can have lives filled with praise and thanksgiving.

PRAISING AT ALL TIMES?
GIVING THANKS IN EVERY SITUATION?

A life of praise may appeal to you. But what does it involve? You may be puzzled about what it means to praise continually and give thanks always, in every situation. Won't this lead to denying your true feelings? Does it mean that when you stub your toe or hit your thumb with a hammer, your spontaneous response must be "Thank You, Lord"? Isn't it dishonest to give thanks if you don't feel thankful?

Several things have helped settle these questions for me.

One is that the Bible doesn't command us to feel thankful in every situation. It doesn't command us to manufacture positive feelings. Instead, it commands us to give thanks (1 Thessalonians 5:18). As Dr. John G. Mitchell, cofounder of Multnomah School of the Bible, put it: "To give thanks when you don't feel like it is not hypocrisy; it's obedience."

This does not mean you should deny your negative thoughts and feelings and attitudes, sweeping them under some inner emotional rug. It doesn't mean you should repress them into some deep cavern where, again and again, they can sneak back into your thoughts, press you into unwise choices, and filter past your defenses to pollute the emotional atmosphere around you.

Notice that David and the other psalmists were honest about their feelings, facing them and telling God about them. They knew how to pour out their hearts before Him (Psalm 62:8). Often they praised God first, and then expressed their disturbed emotions, their perplexities, even their complaints. After this they went on to praise God again, despite their struggles. They did not deny their feelings or simply ignore them. Nor did they wallow in them until they'd all but drowned. And it doesn't seem that they postponed their praise until they had worked through their emotions and felt better. Instead, they mingled an honest pouring-out of their feelings with sincere, God-honoring praise.

Take, for example, Psalm 42. The psalmist composed this song in a time of exile and oppression, when he felt deeply disturbed and downcast. People were saying, "Where is your God—why doesn't He do something for you if He's the true and living God?" The psalmist told God how troubled his heart was. But even as he did so, he honored God, speaking of Him as "the living God...my God...the God of my life...God my rock...the help of my countenance." His every reference to God showed his desire to exalt and glorify Him. And he assured his soul that the time would come when he could once again join the festal worship in the house of God, and praise the Lord for deliverance. Psalm 43, written in a similar situation, likewise honors God in very special ways: "O God...the God of my strength...God my exceeding joy...my God."

What happens when we follow the example of the psalmists—when we express our impressions and feelings, yet choose to keep praising in spite of how things seem to us? I find that sooner or later (often sooner) the Lord releases me from being a slave to my distressing emotions. He unties the tight knots within me and settles my feelings, though He may not answer my questions about how He's handling my affairs. And when at times praise does not quickly bring inner freedom and joy, I can say, "Lord, I can't praise You in the same way I did last week (or last year). I can't seem to respond to You with the same sense of delight and celebration. But I do choose to lift You high, praising You for what You are and what You mean to me."

Life—and praise—isn't always a feast of pure, simple gladness. Don't you find that in many situations you can experience both pleasant and unpleasant emotions? Like Paul, you can be "sorrowful yet always rejoicing" (2 Corinthians 6:10). You can groan and suffer in this fallen world, yet you can learn to rejoice. You can learn to triumph in your hope, in your tribulations and the good things they produce in your life—and above all, in God Himself (Romans 8:22–23; 5:2, 3, 11).

YOU HAVE SUPERNATURAL HELP!

Another help in our worship (perhaps the major one) is the Holy Spirit, that wonderful Gift sent by our risen Lord to indwell us and empower us. The Lord has not set before us the ideal of a life filled with praise and then left us alone to achieve it. How could we, on our own, reach such a high goal—with the down-pull of our old fleshly patterns of living; with the pain of our trials, large or small; with our tendency to depend on ourselves and get distracted from the Lord and do our own thing? But we have the Holy Spirit! Just think of what this means!

He is within you as a fountain of water, springing up to fill you with fresh life—life that is eternal, life that is full. Through Him, time after time, you can know the refreshment that comes from the presence of the Lord. Through the Spirit you can understand the Scriptures and experience the marvelous things God has freely given you in Christ. Through Him you are linked in vital oneness with the Father and the Son, and have all you need for life and godliness. You have all you need to inspire praise: comfort, encouragement, inexpressible joy, overflowing hope, strength in your innermost being, and power to love and serve.

You also have power to praise and give thanks: "Ever be filled with the Spirit...continue giving thanks for everything" (Ephesians 5:18, 20, Williams). You don't have to beg the Holy Spirit to fill you; He is eager to do so. You don't have to earn His fullness, proving you are worthy of it. You have only to let the Spirit fill you...to consent to live under His gracious influence and control. He then performs His amazing ministries in you. Among them: He inspires, reminds, and enables you to worship and praise and give thanks.

Praise Needs Cultivating

If God invites us to praise Him, if praise so enriches our experience of Him, and if we have the Holy Spirit indwelling us, why do we so easily neglect it? Why aren't we at all times attracted to praise as bees are to honey?

I have worshiped the Lord for many years; I know how delightful praise is and how much it stimulates my faith. So why do I ever get so busy, even in my quiet time, that I bypass the delightful opportunity to extol and adore my wonderful Lord? Why do I, time and again, get so busy and absorbed with the pressures of daily life that I forget all about praise? And why do I at times feel reluctant to praise in the midst of everyday trials: when I hear news that makes me anxious about someone I love, or when I face a major disappointment, or when I'm angry or under a lot of pressure?

Could it be that one of Satan's major strategies is to divert us from praise? After all, he knows that God delights in our praise, and that doesn't exactly make him happy. He also detests the rich benefits praise brings to us and others. Or is it simply that our flesh prevails over our spirits, dampening our desire to glorify God? Might it be some of both?

Whatever the reason, we need to pray about a lifestyle of praise as Horatio Bonar did a century ago:

Fill Thou my life, O Lord my God,
In every part with praise,
That my whole being may proclaim
Thy being and Thy ways.
Not for the lip of praise alone,
Nor e'en the praising heart
I ask, but for a life made up
Of praise in every part.[3]

Or as the songwriter, Robert Robinson, prayed in "Come, Thou Fount":

Come, Thou Fount of ev'ry blessing,
Tune my heart to sing Thy grace;
Streams of mercy, never ceasing,
Call for songs of loudest praise.

In spite of all that God has provided, including the Holy Spirit's presence and power, we don't automatically praise and give thanks. Nor will you find praise all of a sudden springing up in full bloom as soon as you start praying about it. Praise flourishes as you weed and water and fertilize your spiritual garden in which it grows. It becomes more constant as you nurture your soul on God's Word and walk in His ways, depending upon the Holy Spirit. It gets richer and more spontaneous as you grow in your knowledge of how worthy the Lord is to receive honor and glory and praise.

But even then praise does not automatically flow from your life day after day, hour after hour. You must choose to cultivate the habit of praise, taking steps that will enrich your praise life.

As you use part 2, "31 Days of Praise," you'll find that praising God is an exciting adventure that yields rich dividends. The praise readings will help you make sense out of the hard realities of life. And—best of all—they'll deepen your experience of how vastly wonderful God is...how loving...how able to satisfy your heart and meet your deepest needs.

How to Use the Praise Pages

You'll find each day of praise in part 2 a rich way to start your quiet time and to end your day, reviewing each reading before bedtime. Underline the phrases that most touch your heart. Also put a mark by the things you need to accept with thanksgiving though you do not feel like it. Ask the Lord to do a special work in your heart in these areas.

Your response to some of the topics of praise may be, "How can I thank the Lord for that?" If these are your feelings, don't decide: "I guess these praise pages aren't for me." Instead, pray about your response. If it's simply a matter of applying what you've learned from the Scriptures differently, feel free to express your praise in other words. But if you find an emotional block in your heart, seek to open yourself to the Lord on the issue that troubles you.

In case He is putting His finger on something important, come back to that day of praise often, asking Him to do a new work within you.

Each reading includes a list of the Scriptures quoted or referred to for that day. The verses are listed by paragraph in the order they occur. You can become enriched and refreshed by meditating on these Scriptures, either before or after your time of praise.

Most Scripture references are taken from the *New American Standard Bible,* although other key versions are noted in parentheses. (See copyright page for complete list of versions and their abbreviations.)

You can use the extra space on the pages for things that will make your praise more personal and refreshing, such as:

— Bible verses or parts of verses

Look up the Scripture references for that day and meditate on them. Write out the passages that mean the most to you, along with any other special verses or thoughts that bless you. You can also use these Bible verses for small group study and discussion. You may find it helpful to look up the verses in two versions: in a more literal translation, such as the King James, New American Standard, or the New International Version; and in a freer translation, such as the New Century Version or the New Living Translation.

— Facts about your life situation

Add personal items that will make your praise and thanksgiving broader, more meaningful to you—both enjoyable things and those issues you find difficult or painful. They will remind you to let God into your inner experience in new ways month after month.

Use the praise pages in an unhurried way, pausing now and then to let your heart quietly appreciate, adore, or stand in awe of your wonderful Lord. Take time to delight in who God is and bask in the sunshine of His presence.

Don't wait until after you've enjoyed all the praise pages to read parts 3 and 4. From the start, begin to read pages 113 through 154. You'll learn more about the rich and exciting ways your adventure in praise will reward you—a powerful enticement to continue praising month after month.

You'll also find answers to some of your questions. And you'll gain insights that will add to your delight in many of the things you'll be praising the Lord for as you go through the days of praise.

Also, you'll want to turn often to page 151, "Your Most Basic Act of Worship," to renew your commitment to our wonderful Lord.

You may also enjoy using the days of praise with your partner, family or roommate, or for small group study and discussion.

I have personalized most of the quotations in these pages, including those from the Bible, to help you use them in praise more easily. In the same way, you may also want to personalize the verses you add.

My longing is that the Lord will use these

thirty-one days of praise to help you—and me—in three ways: to experience God more fully in the varied needs and situations of our lives, to be an increasing joy to Him, and to bring glory to His name in new ways.

1.   A. W. Tozer, *The Pursuit of God* (Harrisburg, Penn.: Christian Publications, Inc., 1948), 20.

2.   Dr. and Mrs. Howard Taylor, *Hudson Taylor's Spiritual Secret* (London, Philadelphia, Toronto, Melbourne, and Shanghai: China Inland Mission, 1935), 122.

3.   Horatio Bonar, "Fill Thou My Life," *Christian Worship* (Exeter, England: The Paternoster Press, 1976), 18.

D A Y

1

Scripture References (by paragraph)

1. Psalm 27:5; 71:3; 91:1–2; Matthew 6:25–26; Psalm 23:1–3;
   Isaiah 62:5b; Zephaniah 3:17–18; Psalm 16:5–6; 107:9

2. Psalm 57:2; 138:8; 86:5; 103:8; Matthew 22:37;
   Jeremiah 32:41; Psalm 37:4; 36:7; 63:7

My heart rejoices in You, Lord, for You are my strong shelter in times of trouble and danger and stress, my hiding place to whom I may continually resort...my Father who lovingly provides for me...my Shepherd who guides and protects me...my Champion who upholds my cause as His child and defends my highest interests...my Bridegroom who delights in me...my God who is mighty to save, who rests in His love for me and rejoices over me with singing, with shouts of joy. You are my inheritance, my share in life, the One who satisfies my longing soul and fills my hungry soul with goodness.

I praise You for Your love and Your wisdom. You are too wise to ever make a mistake, too loving to ever do anything unkind. You act on my behalf, accomplishing what concerns me and fulfilling Your

He who dwells in the shelter of the Most High will abide in the shadow of the Almighty. I will say to the LORD, "My refuge and my fortress, My God, in whom I trust!"

PSALM 91:1-2

purpose for me as I call on You. Thank You that You love me deeply and tenderly. You are compassionate and gracious, full of lovingkindness, ready to forgive, patiently considerate, and generous beyond imagining. You desire my love and rejoice to do good things for me. You delight to give me the desires of my heart as I delight myself in You. How precious is Your love to me, O God! I sing for joy as I take refuge in the shadow of Your wings!

D A Y
2

Scripture References (by paragraph)

1. John 3:16; Galatians 4:4; Hebrews 1:3; Luke 4:18–19; Matthew 5:3; Luke 1:78

2. Luke 4:22; Matthew 9:36; 15:32; 23:37; 23:13–33; John 13:1

3. Psalm 45:2; Song of Solomon 5:16; Philippians 3:8, Phillips

 Thank You, Father, that You so loved the world that You gave Your one and only Son, our Lord Jesus Christ...that when the time had fully come, He wrapped Himself in human form, being born as a helpless baby in a poor family. Thank You that He walked here on earth radiating the brightness of Your glory and flawlessly expressing Your nature...and so, through Him, people saw You in action, involved with them, available to meet their needs. Thank You that He focused Your almighty power into the lives of common people with deep needs, just like me...that He preached the gospel to the poor, proclaimed freedom to prisoners of sin and recovery of sight to the blind, and set free the oppressed victims of sin and Satan—the downtrodden, the lost, the hurting, the broken. Thank You for the way He rebuked the arrogant and looked with favor on the humble-minded,

opening wide the door of His kingdom to those who were destitute and helpless in spirit. I delight in Your tender mercies, O my God, by which the Sunrise from on high has come to us!

Thank You that through the Gospels I can watch this beloved One walk among ordinary people. I can hear the gracious words that came from His lips. I can see His compassion and tenderness toward needy people, His anger at hypocrisy, His faithfulness, His intense love for His followers.

Fairest Lord Jesus! You alone are my heart's desire...my chief delight...my soul's glory, joy, and crown. Every advantage life can offer is like rubbish, compared with the overwhelming gain of knowing You. You are worthy, Lord—worthy to be thanked and praised and worshiped and adored.

D A Y

3

Scripture References (by paragraph)

1. Hebrews 4:12; Matthew 7:24–28; Psalm 40:8; Mark 1:35;
   Luke 5:16; Isaiah 50:4; John 5:19; 6:57; 14:10

2. John 15:5; 1:14, NIV; 2 Corinthians 3:18; Hebrews 13:21;
   2 Thessalonians 2:17; Philippians 1:20, Phillips

 I praise You that the Lord Jesus lived His life sinlessly, in total accord with reality, with no falseness, no self-deception, no dark secrets, nothing to regret, nothing to be ashamed of...that He proclaimed the truth, the one utterly reliable foundation for our thinking and living. Thank You that He delighted to do Your will...that He withdrew for time alone in Your presence...that He was attentive to Your voice and sensitive to Your working...that He lived in complete dependence on You, so that You in Him spoke those gracious and life-giving words and performed those mighty works.

Thank You that He demonstrated how I am to live and serve, completely depending on Him as my indwelling Lord, focusing on His life as He walked on earth, and beholding His glory, "the glory of the

*B*ut we all, with unveiled face beholding as in a mirror the glory of the Lord, are being transformed into the same image from glory to glory, just as from the Lord, the Spirit.

2 CORINTHIANS 3:18

one and only" who came from You, full of grace and truth. What a delight to know that as I focus on Him, You transform me into His image by Your Spirit within me. You work in me that which is pleasing in Your eyes. You strengthen my heart in every good work and every good word, so that more and more I honor Christ by the way I live.

D A Y

4

Scripture References (by paragraph)

1. 1 John 4:10; Philippians 2:6–9; Isaiah 53:3–12;
   2 Corinthians 5:21

2. Acts 2:24; Romans 4:25, NIV; Ephesians 1:20–22,
   Phillips; Hebrews 8:1; 7:25

3. Revelation 1:18; 5:12

 I love You, Father, because You first loved me and sent Your Son to atone for my sins. And I stand amazed that Jesus, who by nature had always been God, did not cling to His rights as Your equal...that He laid aside all His privileges, to be born as a human being...that He totally humbled Himself, submitting to the death of a common criminal, enduring infinite humiliation and pain...that on the cross You laid on Him the compressed weight of all my sin and guilt and shame, of all my griefs and sorrows, and He became sin for me, dying the death I deserved.

And how much I praise You that it was impossible for death to hold Him in its power...that You raised Him from the dead to be my Savior, to make me righteous in Your sight...that You highly exalted Him, giving Him a position infinitely

"And God raised Him up again, putting an
end to the agony of death, since it was
impossible for Him to be held in its power."

A C T S   2 : 2 4

superior to any conceivable command, authority,
power, or control, both natural and supernatural.
Thank You that He is the Great High Priest...that
He is able to save me completely, for He lives forever
and prays for me, and for all of us who have come to
You through Him. I glorify You, my Father, with
gratefulness and joy.

And I bow at the feet of Him who was dead,
and is now alive forever and ever. I exalt Him, I
yield myself to Him, for He is worthy of the total
response of my entire being: "Worthy is the Lamb
that was slain to receive power and riches and
wisdom and might and honor and glory and
blessing."

This is a good time to begin using "Your Most Basic
Act of Worship," which you'll find on page 151.

D A Y

5

Scripture References (by paragraph)

1. Psalm 145:3, 5–6; Ephesians 3:20; Jeremiah 32:17, NKJV; Exodus 15:11

2. Hebrews 1:3; Jeremiah 32:27, NIV; 10:6–7

3. Daniel 5:23d; Isaiah 46:4; Hebrews 13:5

     I magnify You, O Lord, I exalt Your name, for You are great and highly to be praised. I praise You for the glorious splendor of Your majesty and the power of Your awe-inspiring acts. Your power is unlimited...absolute...beyond imagining. You are able to do immeasurably more than we can ask or dream of. "There is nothing too hard for You." Who is like You, "majestic in holiness, awesome in praises, working wonders"?

     O Lord Most High, You rule over the heavens and the earth, for You made all things by Your great power, and You keep them existing and working by Your mighty Word. You are exalted high above every star and galaxy in the entire cosmos...yet You are also "the God of all mankind," the great, personally present, personally involved God who

*T*here is none like Thee, O Lord;
Thou art great, and great is Thy name in
might.

loves, rescues, and takes care of all who trust You.
You exercise Your gracious authority over all
nations—and over each individual in all the world.
There is none like You, the true God, the living
God, the everlasting King.

I praise You for Your sovereignty over the
broad events of my life and over the details. With
You, nothing is accidental, nothing is incidental, and
no experience is wasted. You hold in Your own
power my breath of life and all my destiny. And
every trial that You allow to happen is a platform on
which You reveal Yourself, showing Your love and
power, both to me and to others looking on. Thank
You that I can move into the future nondefensively,
with hands outstretched to whatever lies ahead, for
You hold the future and You will always be with me,
even to my old age...and through all eternity.

D A Y

6

Scripture References (by paragraph)

1. Psalm 99:3, 9; Daniel 4:37; Romans 14:12; Deuteronomy 32:4; Isaiah 2:10–12; Romans 12:19; Hebrews 6:10

2. 1 Thessalonians 4:16; 1 Corinthians 15:51–52; 2 Thessalonians 1:6–10, Phillips; Romans 8:18, Phillips

3. Isaiah 9:6–7; Daniel 4:34; Hebrews 12:28; 1 Timothy 6:15; Revelation 19:6; 1:6

I magnify You, my God, for Your absolute purity, holiness, and justice, as the Judge to whom all people must give account. I praise You that Your fairness is intertwined with everything You do...that when the time is ripe You will end all sin and injustice, all corruption, all immorality...that You will right all wrongs and reward all loving service and suffering for Your sake.

Thank You that Your Son will return from heaven with a shout of triumph, that the dead in Christ will be raised imperishable...and in a flash, in the twinkling of an eye, we shall all be utterly changed. We shall see the radiance of His face and the glorious majesty of His power. It will be a breathtaking wonder and splendor unimaginable to all who believe! Thank You that "whatever we

*B*ehold, I tell you a mystery; we shall not all sleep, but we shall all be changed....

1 CORINTHIANS 15:51

may have to go through now is less than nothing compared with the magnificent future" You have planned for us.

What a joy it is to know that the government will be on Christ's shoulders, and that there will be no end to the increase of His government and peace...that His kingdom will be established with justice and righteousness from then on and forevermore. Your kingdom is an everlasting kingdom...a kingdom that cannot be shaken. You will never be voted out; no coup will ever dethrone You. For all eternity You are the King of kings and Lord of lords. To You be the glory and the dominion forever and ever. Amen!

Scripture References (by paragraph)

1. Isaiah 55:8–11; Psalm 119:11

2. 2 Peter 1:20–21; 2 Timothy 3:16–17

I glorify You for the Bible—that wonderful, written revelation of You and Your plan. As snow and rain fall from the skies to meet our needs, so You have condensed Your thoughts—which are vastly higher than all human thoughts—into written-down form. I'm so grateful that You cared enough to communicate with us in this clear, unchanging, always-accessible way, so that Your thoughts are now available at all times to refresh and nourish and teach me...and that You are still a communicating God, speaking these words to me as I am attentive to You, as I read and meditate with a listening heart. What a privilege it is to store Your Word in my heart, where You can use it at any

$\mathscr{A}$ll Scripture is inspired by God and profitable for teaching, for reproof, for correction, for training in righteousness; that the man of God may be adequate, equipped for every good work.

2 TIMOTHY 3:16–17

moment to bless me and guide me...to keep me from sinning against You...and to be a storehouse of inspired words that the Spirit can bring to my mind to help others.

Thank You that in Your Word I can see Your face and hear Your voice. I can discover Your will and Your patterns for living and serving. I can develop deeper faith and confidence. Thank You that the Holy Spirit inspired Your Word and uses it to enlighten and guide me, and to change me more and more into Your image, from one degree of glory to another.

D A Y

8

Scripture References (by paragraph)

1. Psalm 139:13–16

2. Ephesians 1:6, 12; Romans 12:3–6; Psalm 119:67, 71

3. Psalm 119:73

4. Psalm 95:6

 I give thanks to You, O Lord, and I stand in awe of You, for I am wonderfully made. Marvelous are Your works! Thank You that You uniquely designed and created me, with the same care and precision You used in creating the universe...that You formed me in love exactly to Your specifications...that You embroidered me with great skill in my mother's womb.

I'm grateful that my looks, my abilities, and my personality are like a special picture frame in which You can portray Your grace and beauty, Your love, Your strength, Your faithfulness, to the praise of Your glory. I rejoice that You have gifted me for the special purposes You have in mind for my life. I thank You for Your loving wisdom in allowing the things that have influenced me throughout my life—

*F*or Thou didst form my inward parts;
Thou didst weave me in my mother's womb.
I will give thanks to Thee, for I am fearfully
and wonderfully made; wonderful are Thy
works, and my soul knows it very well.

PSALM 139:13-14

the things that have prepared my heart to respond
to You and live for Your glory. I might not have
turned to You if things had been different!

It's wonderful to know that You are not the
least bit dissatisfied with my inborn talents,
intelligence, aptitudes, appearance, and personality,
for Your hands have made and fashioned me. I am
one of Your original masterpieces!

I worship and bow down; I kneel before You,
my Maker.

Scripture References (by paragraph)

1. Genesis 1:31, 27; Psalm 8:3–6; Isaiah 43:7

2. John 3:27; I Corinthians 4:7; Romans 12:3–6; I Peter 4:10; Romans 11:36; Psalm 115:1, NIV

 I worship before You, dear Lord, as the all-wise Creator, the One who made heaven and earth and all that is in them, and saw that it was very good. I praise You for the honor of being made in Your image, personally formed by You for Your glory, and gifted spiritually just as it has pleased You. Thank You for each strength and ability and desirable trait You have given me. Surely You have been good to me, O Lord!

Thank You that I can enjoy my strengths and gifts without pride or false modesty as I give You the credit for them, praising You rather than congratulating myself. What do I have, that I did not receive from You?...All that I am and all that I have comes from You; it is all sustained by You...and I want it all to glorify You! Not to me, O Lord, not to me, but to Your name be the glory.

When I consider Thy heavens,
the work of Thy fingers,
The moon and the stars, which
Thou hast ordained;
What is man, that Thou dost take
thought of him?
And the son of man, that Thou
dost care for him?
Yet Thou hast made him a little
lower than God,
And dost crown him with glory
and majesty!

PSALM 8:3–5

I specifically thank You for:

D A Y
10

Scripture References (by paragraph)

1. Hebrews 4:15; Romans 8:28–29

2. James 4:6; Psalm 40:17; 2 Corinthians 3:5

3. 2 Corinthians 12:7–10

 I choose to thank You for my weaknesses, my infirmities, my inadequacies (physical, mental, emotional, relational)...for the ways I fall short of what people view as ideal...for my feelings of helplessness and inferiority, and even my pain and distresses. What a comfort it is to know that You understand the feeling of my weaknesses!...and that in Your infinite wisdom You have allowed these in my life so that they may contribute to Your high purposes for me.

I specifically thank You for:

*T*herefore I am well content with weaknesses, with insults, with distresses, with persecutions, with difficulties, for Christ's sake; for when I am weak, then I am strong.

2 CORINTHIANS 12:10

Thank You that many a time my weaknesses cut through my pride and help me walk humbly with You...and then, as You've promised, You give me more grace—You help and bless and strengthen me. Thank You for all the ways I'm inadequate, for they prod me to trust in You and not in myself...and I'm grateful that my adequacy comes from You, the all-sufficient God who is enough!

Thank You that I can trust You to remove or change any of my weaknesses and handicaps and shortcomings the moment they are no longer needed for Your glory, and for my good, and for the good of other people...and that in the meantime, Your grace is sufficient for me, for Your strength is made perfect in my weakness.

Scripture References (by paragraph)

1. Isaiah 46:3; 46:9, 10; Psalm 139:16; Isaiah 63:9; 53:4

2. 1 Corinthians 10:13; 1 Peter 5:9; Genesis 37; 50:17–20

3. 1 Thessalonians 5:18

4. Isaiah 63:9; 53:4

 Thank You, my gracious and sovereign God, that You have been with me and carried me from the day of my birth until today...that You have known my whole life, from beginning to end, since before I was born...and that You wrote in Your book all the days that You ordained for me before one of them came to be.

Thank You that in Your gracious plan to bless and use me, You've allowed me to go through hard times, through trials that many people go through in this fallen world. How glad I am that You're so good at reaching down and making something beautiful out of even the worst situations! How encouraged I am when I think how You did this for Joseph...how his brothers hated and abused and betrayed him, and how You worked these things out for blessing,

*O*n everything give thanks; for this is God's will for you in Christ Jesus.

1 THESSALONIANS 5:18

both for Joseph and his family and for countless other people.

I praise You that the things that happened in my past, both enjoyable and painful, are raw materials for blessings, both in my life and in the lives of others. So I thank You for the specific family (or lack of family) into which I was born and the opportunities You did or did not provide. And thank You for the things in my past that appear to be limitations, hindrances, bad breaks...the wounds of old hurts, the unmet emotional needs, the mistakes or neglect of other people—even their cruelty to me, their abuse.

How comforting to know that in all my distresses You were distressed. And how I thank You, Lord Jesus, that on the cross You bore my griefs

Scripture References (by paragraph)

5. Deuteronomy 8:3; Psalm 66:6–12; 1 Timothy 6:15, Phillips

6. 2 Corinthians 4:17–18

and carried my sorrows, as well as my sins...that I can kneel at the cross and worship You as the One who took on Yourself all my pain and experienced it to the full. And how comforting to know that in the present, day by day, You feel with me any pain, confusion, inner bondage, or struggles that stem from my past. Thank You that all these seeming disadvantages are a backdrop for the special, unfolding plan You have in mind for me...and that if my past still handicaps me, You are able to lead me to the kind of help I need.

I'm so grateful that all my past circumstances were permitted by You to make me see my need of You and prepare my heart for Your Word...to draw me to Yourself, and to work out Your good purposes for my life. I rejoice that You are the Blessed Controller of all things—You are now, You will be

$\mathcal{S}$urely our griefs He Himself bore,
And our sorrows He carried.

ISAIAH 53:4

throughout the future, and You always were. All my days had Your touch of love and wisdom, whether or not I can as yet fully see it.

And Lord, I choose to look beyond my past and present troubles in this life—this temporary life—and fix my eyes on the unseen things that will last forever. I praise You for the eternal glory these things are piling up for me as I choose to trust You.

You'll find further help for trusting God with your past in "Through Praise You Can Strengthen Your Faith," page 113.

Scripture References (by paragraph)

1. 1 Corinthians 1:30; 2 Corinthians 5:21; Romans 5:1;
   Isaiah 53:6; Colossians 2:14, Laubach

2. Romans 14:12; Psalm 50:6; 96:13; Romans 8:1, 33,
   Phillips

3. Hebrews 10:14; Titus 3:4–5; John 13:10;
   Romans 7:18–20, 25; Psalm 130:3–4

 I glory in Your holy name, dear Lord, for in Christ I am righteous with His righteousness. I am justified—just as if I'd never sinned! I'm totally right with You!... Thank You that on the cross Jesus bore all the guilt of all my sins, including past and present and future ones. How grateful I am that, because of what Jesus did, "You crossed out the whole debt against me in Your account books. You nailed the account book to the cross, and closed the account."

Now, Father, I bow before You as the Judge to whom I am accountable as the final Authority, the Chief Justice of the Supreme Court of all the earth...and I thank You, I praise You that You have said—and Your Word cannot be broken—"No

$\mathscr{H}$e made Him who knew no sin to be sin on our behalf, that we might become the righteousness of God in Him.

2 CORINTHIANS 5:21

condemnation now hangs over the head of those who are in Christ Jesus. The judge himself has declared us free from sin."

How I rejoice that through Christ I am all right as a person, now and forever: totally clean, every stain removed...totally forgiven, no matter how great or recent a failure I've had to confess, or how often I have failed.

What amazing grace! What undeserved acceptance and favor! How wonderful that You ask me to do absolutely nothing to earn Your forgiveness—no striving to measure up, no self-punishment, no prolonged remorse, no self-blame, no deeds of penance...that I don't have to sink down into regrets, or into shame, or into denial, or into

Scripture References (by paragraph)

4. Ephesians 2:8—9; Psalm 103:10—14;
   Romans 4:7—8; 11:6; 6:1—2; Ephesians 2:10

5. Isaiah 61:10

excuses for things I do wrong. I'm so thankful that You don't hold a pair of scales and ask me to pile up enough good works to outweigh my sins, my failures, my unworthiness...that it's all by grace through faith. What an incentive to live a life that pleases You, that brings You joy and not grief!

I greatly rejoice in You, Lord; my soul exults in You; for You have clothed me with the garments of salvation, You have wrapped me with a robe of righteousness and beauty, as a bridegroom dressed for his wedding, as a bride adorned with her jewels.

*H*e has not dealt with us according
to our sins,
Nor rewarded us according to our iniquities.
For as high as the heavens are
above the earth,
So great is His lovingkindness toward those
who fear Him.
As far as the east is from the west,
So far has He removed our
transgressions from us.
Just as a father has compassion on his
children,
So the LORD has compassion on those who
fear Him.

PSALM 103:10–13

D A Y

13

Scripture References (by paragraph)

1. Ephesians 1:4; John 6:44; Ephesians 1:6, KJV; John 17:23; Hosea 11:3; Isaiah 43:4

2. Colossians 1:12; Jeremiah 31:3; Romans 8:38–39; Psalm 139:1–6

3. 1 John 3:1; Isaiah 43:4

 I magnify You with thanksgiving, my Father, for I belong to You forever. You chose me in Christ before the creation of the world. You drew me to Yourself. You accepted me in Your beloved Son, welcoming me into the everlasting love You have for Him...and now as Your child You take me in Your arms and tell me that You love me.

> Near, so very near to You
> Nearer I could not be,
> For in the Person of Your Son
> I'm just as near as He!
>
> Dear, so very dear to You,
> I could not dearer be;
> The love wherewith You loved
>   Your Son,
> Such is Your love for me!*

*S*ee how great a love the Father has bestowed upon us, that we should be called children of God; and such we are.

1 JOHN 3:1

Thank You that I have a place in You and Your Kingdom that is eternal...that nothing can separate me from Your limitless, intensely personal love—the one love that is not the least bit based on how much I deserve it, the one love that can never lessen or fail. Thank You that You will never be disillusioned with me, for You already know all about me: past, present and future.

How great is Your love toward me, Father, that I should be called Your child; and such I am. How amazing that I am precious in Your eyes, and that You love me!

*Adapted from *A Mind at Perfect Peace* by Catesby Pagent

Scripture References (by paragraph)

1. Romans 8:9–10; Ephesians 3:16–19

2. Galatians 2:20; 6:14; Romans 6:1–11

3. 2 Corinthians 13:3, Phillips; Philippians 4:13; Romans 8:37

 Father, I'm so glad that the Holy Spirit is within me, to strengthen me with power in my inner person...to make Christ real within me and flood my heart with His limitless love...to fill me with Your fullness...to enable me to know in personal experience the things You have so freely bestowed on me in Christ—my new identity, my incredible spiritual blessings.

I celebrate the fact that I have been crucified with Christ, and that now I am alive with His life...that through my new birth I died out of my old life, and that You resurrected me to a living relationship with You...and so I am dead to sin and alive to You! Thank You that these facts are true, whether or not they seem logical, whether or not I feel they're true...and that as I praise You for them, Your Spirit enables me more and more to live in the

*B*ut may it never be that I should boast,
except in the cross of our Lord Jesus Christ.

light of my new identity in You. Thank You that He is
using Your Word to deliver me from the viewpoints
and values of the world, the flesh, and the devil...and
He is renewing my mind to see things from Your
point of view, so that I can walk in newness of life.

I praise You that Christ is not a weak person
outside me, but a tremendous power inside me...that
through Him I am competent to cope with life, to
do Your will, to love with Your love, to be more than
a conqueror. How I rejoice that I can grow, develop
my gifts, enlarge my capacities...that I need not be
forever shackled by my past, but that with
confidence and joy I can look forward to actually
becoming all that You have in mind for me to be.

Now is a good time to give some thought to
"Praise Can Help You Experience Christ As Your
Life," page 126.

Scripture References (by paragraph)

1. John 15:5; Philippians 2:13

2. Hebrews 10:24–25; Ephesians 4:16, TLB; John 6:35;
   7:37–38; 8:12; Isaiah 9:6; 28:29

3. Isaiah 11:2; John 16:13; Galatians 5:22–23;
   Ephesians 5:18–20; Romans 5:5, Phillips;
   Galatians 5:22–23; Ephesians 3:20; 1:19–21

I'm so grateful, Lord, that the Christian life is not a rigorous self-improvement course or a do-it-yourself kit...that it is not a call to prove myself or improve myself by overcoming my own shortcomings and failures, in my own way, by my own resources. Thank You that, instead, You are at work in me and in my situation to break old patterns of thought and action, to create within me both the desire and the power to do Your gracious will...and to make me a joy to You in new ways.

I praise You that "Jesus Christ is able to untangle all the snarls in my soul, to banish all my complexes, and to transform even my fixed habit patterns, no matter how deeply they are etched in my subconscious" (Corrie ten Boom). Thank You for the many ways You use other people to counsel me and help me grow...and yet that Christ Himself

*O*ur adequacy is from God.

2 CORINTHIANS 3 : 5

is the Answer to my hangups, the one Source who
can meet my deepest needs. How I rejoice that He
is wonderful in counsel and mighty in power, and
that He heals from the inside out.

Thank You, too, for the Holy Spirit—the Spirit
of wisdom and understanding, the Spirit of counsel
and strength. I praise You that He is in me to
enlighten me through Your Word, to flush away my
anxieties and fears, my resentments and hostilities,
my guilt and regrets, as water flushes away dirt and
trash...to keep me filled with Himself and to flood
my heart with Your love...to produce through me the
fruit of love, joy, peace, patience, kindness, goodness,
faithfulness, gentleness and self-control...and to
enable me to give thanks for all things as the hours
and days and weeks pass. I rejoice that You are able
to do far more than all I ask or think, according to
Your power that is at work within me—the same
power that raised Jesus from the dead!

DAY
16

Scripture References (by paragraph)

1. Isaiah 43:4; Matthew 11:11; Romans 8:16–17

2. Ephesians 2:6; 1:20–21

3. John 17:3; Matthew 22:37–38; 1 Peter 4:8–11; Isaiah 43:7; John 17:24

4. 2 Corinthians 5:17; Ephesians 2:10; 1 Peter 2:9

 Thank You, dear Lord, that I am honored in Your eyes…that even the person who is least in Your Kingdom is greater in Your sight than the most prominent and successful person ever born. How wonderful that You, the high King of heaven, enthroned far above all other powers in heaven and earth, have bestowed on me the royal dignity of being Your child and heir!

I exult in Your marvelous grace—in Your favor and blessings which I do not deserve—for You have raised me up with Christ and seated me with Him in the heavenly realm, far above any conceivable command, authority, power, or control. You have given me an exalted status in Your Kingdom—in the one realm where being included and honored has any real significance, any lasting value.

The Spirit Himself bears witness with our spirit that we are children of God.

ROMANS 8:16

How grateful I am that You have linked me to the greatest possible purposes, the highest of all reasons for living: to know and love You...to show Your love to other people...to glorify You...and to enjoy You now and forever. What an honor!

Thank You that, in my deepest and truest identity, I am a new person in union with Christ...that I am one of Your spiritual masterpieces, created clean and clear as a flawless jewel...and that You are cutting and polishing me to receive and display more fully the beauty of Your glorious attributes!

Scripture References (by paragraph)

1. Isaiah 46:9; Genesis 37; 39; Psalm 105:16–20; Genesis 50:20; Romans 11:33 (Phillips)

2. Psalm 37:5; 73:24; Revelation 3:7–8

Thank You that You have me in the place You want me just now...that even if I got here through wrong choices or indifference or even rebellion, yet You knew my mistakes and sins before I ever existed, and You worked them into Your plan to draw me to Yourself, to mold and bless me, and to bless others through me. Thank You that, even if I'm here through the ill-will or poor judgment of other people, all is well; for in Your sovereign wisdom You are at work to bring about good results from all those past decisions, those past events beyond my control—good results both for me and for others. Thank You again that You meant for good the terrible things that happened to Joseph, who was sold into slavery, exiled to a distant country, and later sent to prison on false accusations...and

*O*h, the depth of the riches both of the wisdom and knowledge of God! How unsearchable are His judgments and unfathomable His ways!

ROMANS 11:33

that through all this You had him in the right place at the right time, for highly important reasons. I'm glad, Lord, that You are the same today—well able to work things out for us, to turn evil into good. I stand amazed at the complexity and mystery of Your wisdom. How safe it is for me to trust Your reasons for acting (or not acting) and Your methods of working!

Thank You that I can safely commit my location and situation to You. I can "be willing for You to shift me anywhere on life's checkerboard, or bury me anywhere in life's garden, gladly yielding myself for You to please Yourself with, anywhere and anyway You choose" (source unknown). Thank You that I can trust You with my future places— ready to go, ready to stay.

3. Deuteronomy 1:33

4. Psalm 90:1; 91:1; 31:20; 36:7–8; 65:3; 27:4–5;
   John 15:5; Psalm 23:6

So I rest in the fact that You have me in this place for this day, and I praise You that You will faithfully guide me throughout life to just where You want me to be, as I seek to do Your will.

And most important of all is my place in You. How delighted I am to have You as my dwelling place where I can settle down, feel secure and be content anywhere on earth.... You are my blessed home, "where I can enter and be at rest even when all around and above is a sea of trouble" (Andrew Murray). How my soul delights to hide in the secret of Your presence...to take refuge in the shadow of Your wings, to eat at Your table, to drink my fill of the river of Your delights. How blessed I am, my King and my God, for You have chosen me, and

$\mathscr{H}$e who dwells in the shelter of the Most High will abide in the shadow of the Almighty.

PSALM 91:1

brought me near, to live in Your presence, to behold Your delightfulness, to seek Your counsel.... And to think that I will dwell in Your house forever!

It will be worth your while to give some more thought to "Through Praise You Can Profit More from Your Trials," page 123. This will further prepare you for many of the following days of praise.

DAY

18

Scripture References (by paragraph)

1. Romans 8:28–29; I Peter 1:6–7

2. James 1:2–4, Phillips

3. Psalm 68:8–12; 138:7–8; Job 23:10;
   Deuteronomy 8:2–3, 16–17; 2 Corinthians 4:17–18;
   John 12:27–28

 Father, I'm so delighted that You are both loving and sovereign, and that You cause all things to work together for good to those who love You, to those who are called according to Your purpose. So I thank You for each disturbing or humbling situation in my life, for each breaking or cleansing process You are allowing, for each problem or hindrance, for each thing that triggers in me anxiety or anger or pain. And I thank You in advance for each disappointment, each demanding duty, each pressure, each interruption that may arise in the coming hours and days.

In spite of what I think or feel when I get my eyes off You, I choose not to resist my trials as intruders, but to welcome them as friends.

Thank You that each difficulty is an opportunity to see You work...that in Your time You will bring me out to a place of abundance. I rejoice that You plan to enrich and beautify me through each problem, each conflict, each struggle...that through them You expose my weaknesses and needs, my hidden sins, my self-centeredness (and especially my self-reliance and pride). Thank You that You use trials to humble me and perfect my faith and produce in me the quality of endurance...that they prepare the soil of my heart for the fresh new growth in godliness that You and I both long to see in me...and that my momentary troubles are producing for me an eternal glory that far outweighs them all, as I keep my eyes focused on You. I'm grateful that You look beyond my superficial desire for a trouble-free life; instead, You fulfill my deep-down desire to glorify You, enjoy Your warm fellowship, and become more like Your Son.

> I thank You for the bitter things
> They've been a friend to grace,
> They've driven me from the paths
>   of ease
> To storm the secret place.
>
> — FLORENCE WHITE WILLETT

D A Y
19

Scripture References (by paragraph)

1. Philippians 1:3; 1 Thessalonians 2:19–20; Psalm 68:6a;
   Ephesians 4:11–16; Galatians 6:10; Matthew 22:39;
   1 John 4:11–12; Psalm 133:1

 Thank You, Lord, for the people who are a
blessing to me...for family and friends and
neighbors, for little children, for brothers and sisters
in Christ, for colleagues and leaders, for pastors and
teachers...and for others: our doctor, the postman,
the plumber. Thank You for the many ways You use
these people to meet my needs, brighten my path,
and lighten my load...to enrich my knowledge of
You, and to counsel or correct or nourish me,
building me up in the faith. How good and how
pleasant it is to enjoy rich fellowship with those who
love You. Thank You for bringing people into my
life!

$\mathcal{B}$eloved, if God so loved us, we also ought to love one another.... If we love one another, God abides in us, and His love is perfected in us.

1 JOHN 4:11–12

I thank You specifically for:

Scripture References (by paragraph)

2. Isaiah 9:6; Psalm 46:1; 1 John 4:10, 18–19; Psalm 45:2; Hebrews 7:26; Psalm 40:5b

Yet, Lord, I also thank You that even the people I most admire have flaws—that only You are wonderful through and through, with no ugly edges, and that people, even at their best, cannot meet my deepest needs...that at times they misunderstand, they disappoint, they expect too much, or they can't be available when I need them. This makes me even more glad to have You as my best Friend, my wonderful Counselor, my ever-present help in trouble, immediately available around the clock, seven days a week. How wonderful that I belong to You, the pure, unpolluted Source from which all downstream loves flow. So I delight in people here on earth; but first and last I come to You, the only perfect Person, the only ideal Person, the only One

We love, because He first loved us.

1 JOHN 4:19

whose love is flawless...the only One who is worthy
of my highest praise. O God, who is like You? There
is none to compare with You!

I thank You for the friends who've failed
To meet my soul's deep need;
They've driven me to the Savior's feet
Upon His love to feed.

I'm grateful too, through all
    life's way
No one could satisfy,
And so I've found in You alone
My rich, my full supply!

FLORENCE WHITE WILLETT

Scripture References (by paragraph)

1. Romans 8:28–29; 1 Peter 1:6–7; James 1:2–4, Phillips;
    Psalm 27:10; Isaiah 49:14–16; Psalm 142:3–5;
    1 Thessalonians 3:12; Philippians 1:9–11

2. Matthew 5:43–45; Hosea 3:1

3. 1 Peter 2:1; Romans 15:7; Ephesians 4:31–32;
    Matthew 7:1–3; 6:14–15; 18:21–22; Psalm 37:1–7

 Father, I thank You for the people in my life
who seem to bring more pain than joy, for I
believe You have let our paths cross for important
reasons. Thank You for the good things You want to
do in my life through the things that bother me
(their irritating habits? their moodiness? their
unloving ways? their demands? their insensitivity?
their unrealistic expectations?). I'm grateful that
You are with me, to meet my needs when others—
even those close to me—fail to do so. I'm so glad
that You are also within me, working to make me
more like Jesus—more patient, more gentle, more
loving—through the very things I dislike.

Thank You too that You love these people, and
that Your love is adequate to meet their deep needs
and to transform their lives, however willful or
unwise they may sometimes be. Thank You that You

care for them deeply, and that each of them has the potential of being a vast reservoir from which You could receive eternal pleasure. And so, though I may not feel grateful, I give thanks for them by faith, trusting Your goodness, Your wisdom, Your power, and Your love for them as well as for me.

And I praise You that I need not fret about these people, or be envious, or mull over angry thoughts to prove I'm right. Thank You that by Your power I can receive them as You receive me: just as I am, warts and wrinkles and hangups and all...that I can choose not to judge them, but to forgive them...to cancel any debts I feel they owe me—any apologies, any obligations...that through Your grace, I can choose to wipe clean any slate of grievances I have within me, and to view these people with a heart that says, "You no longer owe me a thing." Thank You for Your Spirit who empowers me, so that I can do them good, delight in You, and commit my way to You, resting in You as You unfold Your good purposes in these relationships—in Your time.

Scripture References (by paragraph)

1. Psalm 103:1–2; 128:1–4

2. Psalm 73:25; 45:2; Song of Solomon 5:10; Psalm 16:5–6

3. Psalm 89:5–17; Jeremiah 10:6–7; 2 Corinthians 11:2; Hosea 2:19–20; Isaiah 54:5; Psalm 73:25–26

4. Psalm 107:8–9; 62:3; 84:11; Isaiah 55:1–2

 Thank You, Lord, for each specific strong point and admirable quality in my life partner.* Thank You for bringing us together, and for the way Your love sweetens our earthly love! I bless You, Lord, for the many benefits You have given me through this dear one.

Here are some special reasons I want to thank You for this relationship:

Yet, Lord, I praise You that You far surpass even the best person in my life. You are distinguished above all, "the most winsome of all

$\mathcal{W}$hom have I in heaven but Thee?
And besides Thee, I desire nothing on earth.

PSALM 73:25

beings" (Tozer). You are my share in life, my reward, my inheritance.

Who can compare with You? You are my perfect Life Partner, my dearest, most-delightful Loved One, my always-present Companion. You are the strength of my life, and my portion forever. Only my relationship with You is sure to be lifelong and more, with never a good-bye!

Thank You that "You are so vastly wonderful, so utterly and completely delightful, that You can meet and overflow the deepest demands of my total nature, mysterious and deep as that nature is" (Tozer).

* If you are married, make your partner the topic of your praise. If you are not married, choose another person who is close to you: a family member, roommate, or friend. Give thanks for that person's good qualities—even if right now you find it difficult to focus on those good points.

D A Y

22

Scripture References (by paragraph)

1. 1 Thessalonians 5:18

2. Hebrews 12:10–11

3. Psalm 139:14; Jeremiah 32:17, 27; Romans 4:17; Proverbs 3:5; 1 Peter 3:1–9; Philippians 1:9–10; Galatians 5:22–23

4. James 1:5; Psalm 148:8, 10

 Thank You for Your ultimate good purposes in allowing the weaknesses or failures of the person for whom I praised You in Day Twenty-One (indifference? lack of understanding? harshness? explosiveness? undue need to control? excessive dependence? excessive independence? failure to lead, failure to follow, failure to love? lack of alertness and awareness? other lacks or failures or even grievous sins?).

I especially want to thank You for what You plan to do through the following things that disappoint me, upset me, make me anxious, or break my heart:

Thank You for Your ultimate good purposes in allowing these things. And thank You so much that

*T*o sum up, let all be harmonious, sympathetic, brotherly, kindhearted, and humble in spirit; not returning evil for evil, or insult for insult, but giving a blessing instead.

1 PETER 3 : 8 – 9

these things do not make up the whole picture—that this loved one is also wonderfully made, and has a bright side as well as a dull side. And I rejoice that You are loving and powerful, well able to change this person if and when and as You choose. Thank You that in the meantime You are working to change me through these imperfections that frustrate or grieve me...that my reactions to them throw light on ways I need to grow—to trust You more—and to meet my loved one's needs more fully, as I let the Holy Spirit fill me with Your love and patience and peace.

I rejoice that You are able to empower me in difficult times and to give me wisdom in my responses. You are all-sufficient, more than enough to meet even the deepest needs of my heart, whatever today or the future may bring.

DAY

23

Scripture References (by paragraph)

1. Romans 8:28–29

2. James 1:2–4, Phillips; 2 Chronicles 20:15;
   James 1:5, 19–20; 3:17–18; Ecclesiastes 3:7

3. Psalm 44:4; 119:91, RSV; Isaiah 66:4

4. Psalm 27:13

 Thank You that You plan to use for good
the struggles my loved ones face—including
their disappointing choices, their unwise or even
harmful ways of thinking and living, and their
sidetracks from going Your way (as I see it—and,
Lord, I know I could be wrong!).

I praise You in advance for the part these
difficult things are going to play in Your good plan
for us—in eventual deliverance and growth and
fruitfulness. I'm grateful that in all these things, the
battle is not mine but Yours...and that the final
chapter has not yet been written. How good it is
that I can call on You to give me wisdom to know
what to say or not say, what to do and not do...and
that You live in me so that I can love with Your love,
even when it's hard. Thank You that these trials
force me to trust You more!

$\mathcal{A}$nd we know that God causes all things to work together for good to those who love God, to those who are called according to His purpose.

ROMANS 8:28

I worship before You, my King and my God. I'm grateful that You command victories for Your people...and that "all things are Your servants." You're a God who acts on behalf of the one who puts his hope in You. Thank You that You are at work to answer my prayers in Your good way and time.

Thank You for past victories You have won in my loved ones' lives—for progress and growth and answered prayer—and for the victories we will yet see in the future, to the glory of Your Name. I praise You that as time goes by, in new ways You will show us Your goodness in the land of the living.

Scripture References (by paragraph)

1. Romans 8:28–29; Psalm 61:2

2. Proverbs 3:5; Psalm 37:5; 2 Corinthians 3:18; 1 John 1:9

3. 1 Peter 5:5; Romans 5:5, TLB

 Thank You, my loving and sovereign God, that my failures and mistakes are part of the "all things" You work together for good...as well as my tensions and stresses, my hostile and anxious feelings, my regrets, my trips into shame and self-blame—and the specific things that trigger them. I praise you that "all things," including these, can contribute to my spiritual growth and my experience of You....When my heart is overwhelmed, I'm more aware of my need to cry to You...to take refuge in You...to rely on You.

I rejoice that these things keep reminding me to depend on You with all my heart...that they prompt me to trust in Your love, Your forgiveness, Your power, Your sufficiency, Your ability to overrule, and Your transforming presence within me. Thank You for the ways that my shortcomings

*T*rust in the LORD with all your heart,
and do not lean on your own understanding.

PROVERBS 3 : 5

and failures bring pressure on me to open myself to
You more fully, and the way they let You show me
deep and hidden needs: griefs and hurts that I've
never poured out before You, that I've never
exposed to Your healing touch, and sins that I've
never faced and acknowledged. How grateful I am
for Your constant cleansing as I confess each sin You
make me aware of, and then turn back to You as my
Lord. I praise You that I'm free from condemnation
simply because Christ died for me and rose
again...that it doesn't depend on how well I live.

I praise You for how You use my sins and
failures to humble me, and for how this opens me to
the inflow of Your grace—amazing grace, that
enables me to hold my head high, not in pride but in
humble gratitude for Your undeserved, unchanging
love and total cleansing!

Scripture References (by paragraph)

1. Isaiah 57:15; Galatians 2:6; James 2:1,5;
   1 Corinthians 1:26–29; James 4:6; Psalm 73:18

2. Psalm 103:13–14; Jeremiah 18:3–6

3. 2 Corinthians 4:7

Dear Lord, how much I appreciate Your viewpoint regarding human status and abilities, failures and weaknesses. I'm so glad that You, the high and exalted One, are not impressed with the positions people hold...that You are not in the least partial or prejudiced...that You show no personal favoritism. Thank You that You have no regard for any external distinctions: for rich or poor, for famous or unknown, for high rank or low, for handsome or homely, for any race or culture above any other...but that You do have regard for all who are humble in heart. Thank You that You are not looking for ideal people with imposing lists of human qualifications, but that You use people whom the world calls foolish and weak, poor and insignificant. Thank You that You oppose those who exalt themselves, and that You exalt those who humble themselves, giving them Your grace.

How glad I am that You don't expect perfect performance. "You are quick to mark every simple effort to please You, and just as quick to overlook imperfections when I meant to do Your will" (Tozer). You are full of mercy and compassion toward me. You know the way I'm put together; You know my limitations; You understand that I am dust. And I praise You that You are greater than any or all of my failures...that as my Potter You are able to mold and remold me, as I submit to Your wisdom and skill...that as the Master Artist You are able to take the dark threads of my life—my wounds, my scars, my blotches, the messes I make, and even my sins—and blend them into a beautiful design, to the praise of the glory of Your grace.

Thank You that I, a common earthenware jug, contain the priceless treasure of Your life and glory, and so my every victory and accomplishment obviously comes from Your all-prevailing power, and not from me.

Scripture References (by paragraph)

1. Colossians 2:15; Ephesians 1:19–21; Philippians 2:9–10; Ephesians 2:6

2. 1 John 4:4; Revelation 12:11; Acts 16:18; Ephesians 6:17; Revelation 20:10

3. Isaiah 49:23–25; Psalm 108:13

Father, I praise You that Jesus is Victor over Satan and all his evil powers—that He triumphed over them through the Cross and Resurrection, and that You have highly exalted Him. You have given Him a position infinitely superior to all other powers and authorities...a name that stands far above all other names that will ever be used, and—amazing grace—You have raised me up and enthroned me with Him in the heavenly realms.

How I praise You that I need not strive toward a possible victory, but can live from a position of victory already won—that He who is in me (Father, Son, and Holy Spirit) is greater than he who is in the world...that although Satan is powerful, he cannot prevail against the blood of the Lamb and the Name of our Lord Jesus Christ. Thank You that Satan must retreat before that Name and before

Your Word, the living and powerful sword of the Spirit, and that in the end he will be cast down into everlasting defeat and shame.

What a joy to know that You are the same today as You were centuries ago in Isaiah's day, when You promised to rescue Your people in a hopeless-looking situation, when the enemy seemed to have prevailed. How I love the words You spoke to them: "Those who hopefully wait for Me will not be put to shame.... Even the captives of the mighty man will be taken away, and the prey of the tyrant will be rescued; For I will contend with the one who contends with you, and I will save your sons." I praise You that I can count on You to do this in our spiritual warfare, and that through You we shall do valiantly, for You will trample down our enemies.

"Praise Can Help You Overcome Satan and His Crafty Strategies," page 138, throws further light on experiencing victory over Satan and his helpers.

D A Y
27

Scripture References (by paragraph)

1. Ephesians 1:19–20; 3:20; Luke 1:37

2. Psalm 50:23, NIV

3. Psalm 66:3, NIV; Zechariah 4:6

 Lord, I extol You for Your great power toward us who believe—Your tremendous, invincible power that works in us and for us...the same almighty strength You used when You raised Jesus from the dead and seated Him far above all other powers, visible and invisible. You are able to do infinitely beyond all our highest prayers or thoughts. Nothing is impossible with You!

Thank You that when I praise You and bring my requests to You in simple faith, I plug into Your almighty power...that when I offer a sacrifice of thanksgiving, I open a door for You to rescue me and bless my life, and I prepare the way for You to rescue and bless other people, near and far.

"So great is your power that your enemies cringe before you." I lift my praise to You, for "no human imagination can take in the startling,

"*He* who offers a sacrifice of thanksgiving honors Me...."

PSALM 50:23

revolutionary power, softly, subtly, but with irresistible sweep, that flows down from the crowned Christ among grateful men and women...that flows through the lives of individuals wholly under the gracious influence of the Holy Spirit...through people who simply live in full-faced touch with Christ, and who take that power as the need arises and the sovereign Holy Spirit leads" (adapted from S. D. Gordon). Thank You that I am part of a vast army of people around the world— people who live in full-faced touch with Your Son and move Your mighty hand to bring about Your gracious purposes. Thank You that our influence and our victories are not by human might or power, but by Your Spirit.

Today you may want to meditate on "Through Praise You Can Activate God's Power," page 121.

D A Y

28

Scripture References (by paragraph)

1. Ephesians 3:12; Hebrews 10:19–22; 4:16;
   Ephesians 3:12, TLB; Romans 5:17

2. Philippians 4:6; Psalm 62:8; 1 John 1:8–10;
   Proverbs 28:13

3. Psalm 46:10; Isaiah 40:31; John 4:23;
   Song of Solomon 2:14; 7:10

 I exult in the free, confident access You have provided, so that I can come into Your Presence for warm fellowship, for refreshment, for mercy when I've failed, for grace when I'm in need. What a joy to know that I can draw near to You at any moment, wherever I may be...that I can come boldly to Your throne of grace, assured of Your glad welcome—not because I'm worthy or because I've served You, but because You're a God of grace, a God of unmerited, unlimited favor—not little dribbles of favor reluctantly measured out, but overflowing, superabundant favor. I'm so glad that You welcome me just as I am, simply because Jesus is my risen Savior, and I am alive with His life and righteous with His righteousness!

Thank You that I can praise and adore You and offer my requests in detail, with thanksgiving...that I can pour out my heart before You, being honest with You about my feelings and my mistakes and my sins. Thank You that when I turn to You as my Lord and confess my sins rather than hiding them or clinging to them, Your forgiveness is immediate and total...that I never need to fear that You will judge or condemn me.

Thank You that I can "be still" (cease striving, let go, relax) and know that You are God...that You are in control...and that I can restfully depend upon You and absorb Your strength and joy and peace. To think that You not only permit me to come before You, but You actually desire my fellowship, my worship, my prayers, and my eternal presence! Your desire is for me. "That You should allow Your creature to have fellowship with You is wonderful enough; but that You can desire it, that it gives You satisfaction and joy and pleasure, is almost too much for my understanding."* Thank You.

*The Quiet Time (Downers Grove, Ill.: InterVarsity Press, 1945), 4.

You'll find further help in enjoying God in "Through Praise You Can Tune in God's Enriching Presence," page 119.

DAY
29

Scripture References (by paragraph)

1. Colossians 3:4; 1 Corinthians 12:13; 6:19;
   Ephesians 3:16–19; 1 Peter 2:9

2. Isaiah 53:6; Matthew 11:28–29; Psalm 55:22; 68:19;
   Hebrews 13:20–21; Philippians 4:13

3. Proverbs 3:5–6; Hebrews 13:20–21; Galatians 2:20

4. 1 Peter 5:7, Phillips

 Thank You that Christ is my Life...that I am a member of His body and a dwelling place of His Spirit. How privileged I am to be indwelt by Your glorious presence (by the whole Trinity: Father, Son, and Holy Spirit!) so that You can display Your excellence to those around me.

Thank You for the day when I let go of the whole burden of my sins and rested on the atoning work of Christ—on the total payment He made for me on the cross.... And thank You that today, in that same simple way, I can let go of the whole burden of my life and service...of my marriage, children, and all my relationships (past, present, and future), of my inadequacies and my self-dependence, and rest on Your presence working in me through the Holy Spirit. How good it is to transfer these burdens from my shoulders to Yours, and to rest on You to work in me and for me and through me! I praise You for the gracious way You infuse me with inner strength through Christ...and so I'm ready for anything You want me to do, and I'm equal to anything You allow to happen in my life.

Thank You that I can give myself up to be led by You...that I can go forth praising and at rest, letting You manage me and my day...that I can joyfully depend on You throughout the day, expecting You to guide, to enlighten, to reprove, to teach, to use, and to do in me and with me what You desire...that I can count upon Your working in me and through me as a fact, totally apart from sight or feeling...that I can go forth praising and at rest, believing You and obeying You and ceasing from the burden of trying to manage myself without Your wisdom and power (adapted from Dr. John Hubbard).

Thank You that I can throw the whole weight of my anxieties on You, for I am Your personal concern.

Here's another day of praise where you may want to review "Praise Can Help You Experience Christ As Your Life," page 126.

D A Y

30

Scripture References (by paragraph)

1. Acts 17:24; John 3:16; Galatians 4:5–6; 1 John 2:2; Acts 13:47; Revelation 5:8; 2 Peter 3:9

2. 2 Corinthians 4:6; Ephesians 2:19; Romans 12:4–6; Acts 1:8; Matthew 28:18–20

3. Psalm 57:11, NIV

I worship You, Lord of heaven and earth, the God who made the world and all things in it! I extol You for the immensity of Your love in sending Jesus Christ, the long-awaited Messiah, the Savior who died for us, and for all people everywhere. I exalt You because Your plan embraces the whole world and all of time...not just the Middle East, which cradled the gospel, but also Europe and North America, Asia and Africa, the entire southern hemisphere, and every tiny island on the globe. Thank You that Jesus, with His blood, purchased sons and daughters for You from every tribe and language and people and nation...and that You yearn for all people everywhere to repent; You have no desire that any person should spend eternity without You!

Thank You that You made Your light shine in my heart to give the light of the knowledge of Your glory in the face of Your Son...that You drew me to Yourself, and honored me, making me a member of Your royal family and a citizen of Your Kingdom...and that You have enlisted me in Your worldwide task force, to be Your witness. What a high privilege, that You have destined me to have a share not only in Your love but also in Your glorious purposes, both near and far...that You have gifted me for a unique part in Your global search for people who will repent and believe and learn to live for Your glory. I celebrate my high calling of knowing You and making You known! And I praise You for giving me Your Holy Spirit to fill and empower me, and for promising to be with me always.

"Be exalted, O God, above the heavens; let Your glory be over all the earth."

You'll find additional help on reaching the world—wherever you are now, wherever you'll be in the future—from "Praise Can Help You Demonstrate God's Reality in a Secular, Materialistic Society," page 136.

Scripture References (by paragraph)

1. Psalm 102:25–27; Hebrews 13:8; Jeremiah 31:3;
   Philippians 1:6; 1 Thessalonians 5:24, Phillips

2. 2 Peter 1:4; 1 Kings 8:56; Jeremiah 32:17, 27;
   Romans 4:17–21

3. Jude 24–25, NIV

 I exult before You because You are eternal and never-changing in Your truth, in Your attributes, and in Your attitude toward me and all Your loved ones. I'm so glad that Your persistent tenderness binds my heart to You forever...that You who began a good work in me will carry it to completion until the day of Christ Jesus. You are utterly faithful and will finish what You have set out to do. You will not abandon the work You have begun.

Thank You for giving us priceless promises, great beyond measure—promises that apply to Your work in me, in my loved ones, in my situation, in my service, and in the whole world...and not one single word of Your good promises has ever failed. I glorify You because no human problem, however hopeless or impossible, is too hard for You. You are able to

"*Blessed* be the LORD…according to all that He promised; not one word has failed of all His good promise."

1 KINGS 8 : 5 6

give life to the dead and call into being that which does not exist. So I need not stagger at Your promises or waver in unbelief. What You have promised You are able to perform!

To You who are able to keep us from falling and to present us before Your glorious presence without fault and with great joy—to the only God our Savior be glory, majesty, power, and authority, through Jesus Christ our Lord, before all ages, now and forevermore! Amen.

III

THE IMPORTANCE
OF PRAISE

To assure stick-to-it-iveness in your praise adventure, let's take a further look at the importance of praise. God's Word gives still more reasons why praise is more than an obligation, more than a pleasant extra in your walk with God...why it is not optional, but essential. If you find yourself lagging in your praise journey, come back to the following pages and let the Lord remotivate you.

THROUGH PRAISE YOU CAN STRENGTHEN YOUR FAITH

Praise is a basic way both to express our faith and to strengthen it; and strengthened faith is no small benefit. From cover to cover the Bible shows us that faith—or trust—is the basic response God is looking for. Faith moves God to reveal Himself to us and do His mighty work in us, as well as for us. Faith brings victory that changes our circumstances—or victory in the midst of circumstances that don't change.

It's not that praise is a sort of magical incantation that makes us strong in faith and maneuvers God into doing what we want. Rather, through praise we focus on God. We fix our inner eyes on Him with a basic trust in Him. Our praise springs from this simple response of faith, this simple choice to believe God; and praise in turn increases our confidence in Him.

Time after time Warren and I find that praise is a quick route to an assured faith, a faith that rests in God and counts on Him to work. When in one way or another we slip off the freeway of faith, praise is often the ramp that gets us back on.

Not infrequently we slip into distrust because we're frustrated at file folders stuffed with unfinished paper work—folders that represent unfinished people work.

One night we were taking a prayer walk along the beach that borders the Singapore harbor. Suddenly Warren remembered an urgent letter he had put off writing. Together we plummeted into laments and regrets, anxious about the problems this might cause the couple waiting for his reply.

After our morbid sidetrip, we got back to prayer. We praised God that He was sovereign, that He was almighty, and that He had promised to work in answer to prayer. Then Warren asked Him to overrule this delay and praised Him that somehow He would use it for good.

Praise helped us fix our faith on our merciful, all-powerful God who is infinitely greater than our failures. At first we chose to praise with tiny stirrings of faith. Then God freed us from our unbelief and renewed our confidence in Him. Once more praise had been a ramp onto the highway of faith.

The letter was soon on its way. Weeks later we got a reply from our friends, who wrote, "We wouldn't have been ready for your suggestions a week earlier." God had used the delay to get Warren's letter to them at exactly the right time. More reason for praise!

Through praise you can demonstrate your faith

in God to work in the present as He has in past centuries. Remember the suffering that Joseph went through: the cruel betrayal by his brothers who sold him into a life of slavery, the agonies of his soul, the false accusations, the years in prison, and the forgetfulness of the butler, which meant two extra years of imprisonment. Yet God allowed all these events for good. He used them to prepare Joseph to be prime minister of the greatest nation on earth. Through them, He had Joseph in the right place at the right time to keep hundreds of thousands of people alive—including himself and his family— during a severe and prolonged famine! How did Joseph evaluate all that had happened? He told his brothers, "You meant evil against me, but God meant it for good" (Genesis 50:20).

Through praise you can follow the example of Paul and Silas in Acts 16. They had been beaten and taken to prison, where their feet were placed in stocks. Talk about pain and discomfort and reasons to postpone praise! Yet in that miserable prison they prayed and sang hymns of praise at about midnight; and suddenly the Lord released them through a special earthquake that hit at exactly the right time, in exactly the right place.

Or you can follow Paul's example when he wrote to the Philippians. This time he was in prison for years. Yet he rejoiced in the Lord, confident that his suffering was accomplishing the deep desire of his heart—the progress of the gospel.

In the twenty-first century as in the first, praise can increase our faith and release the transforming power of Christ in us and our situations—as well as in people near us or across the globe from us.

Some years ago I read about a woman who began to thank God for her ex-husband and his alcoholism and for all the years of loneliness and heartache she had experienced. As she continued to praise, she became aware of her own self-righteousness and superior attitude toward him, and of the way she had been a joyless martyr, immersing herself in self-pity. She confessed her sin, acknowledging that her pride was worse than her husband's alcoholism, and kept on praising and rejoicing.

As time went by, this woman's husband, miles away with no direct influence from her, came to Christ and was delivered from his alcoholism. He returned to her and they began a new life together. For this woman, praise helped to change both her and her situation.

Even in troubled circumstances, or when God does not choose to work in spectacular ways, praise can help us view our situation through different lenses. It can help produce within us a restful, invigorating inner climate.

And often this change of climate within us helps transform the atmosphere around us, for our new attitudes cause people to react differently to us. We begin to exert a creative and uplifting influence on them.

So praise brings obvious victory, or it enables us to turn apparent defeats (whether dramatic trials or minor irritations) into victory from God's viewpoint. It tunes out the conflicting voices that shatter our faith and block our love; and it tunes us in to God's guidance so that we can discern what action to take, if any.

True praise is unconditional. It's not an attempt to manipulate God into producing the precise results we hope for. Instead, it helps us accept our situation as it is, whether or not He changes it. Continued praise helps us reach the place where we can say, "Father, I don't want You to remove this problem until You've done all You want to do through it, in me and in others."

THROUGH PRAISE YOU CAN TUNE IN GOD'S ENRICHING PRESENCE

Psalm 22:3 tells us that God inhabits the praises of His people. Some versions say He is "enthroned" upon our praises. When we praise, we enthrone God in our lives and circumstances, and He manifests His presence in a special way.

Much as television waves surround us at all times, so God's presence is always in us and with us, though it may not always be evident. Praise can flip the switch that, so to speak, turns on that mighty, glorious presence and tunes us in to His sufficiency. We become filled to overflowing with Him. Our lives become a stage on which He, the leading Actor, reveals Himself in love and power, blessing both us and the people we relate to.

In 1960 my first husband, Dean Denler, was hospitalized in Hong Kong with terminal cancer. At that point praise took on a new importance in Dean's life. He decided that, through praise, he would make his hospital room a special dwelling place for God.

"I'll be praising God for all eternity," he told me, "but only during my brief time on earth can I bring Him joy through praising Him in the midst of pain."

Some months later a close friend was officiating at Dean's funeral. He told those who had gathered, "Dean's room became a sanctuary, his bed a pulpit, and all who came to comfort him were blessed."

Praise did not bring healing of Dean's cancer. But through praise and faith Dean brought the refreshment of God's presence into a painful situation, honoring God in death as he had in life.

THROUGH PRAISE YOU CAN ACTIVATE GOD'S POWER

As you pray and praise the Lord, you can free God to reveal His power as well as His presence. Prayer has been called "the slender nerve that moves the mighty hand of God" (source unknown). Any form of sincere, believing prayer directs God's power into our lives and situations, but this is especially true of prayer blended with praise.

Your praise and thanksgiving can help form a highway—a smooth, level road—on which the Lord can ride forth unhindered to deliver and bless. We see this in Psalm 68:4, "Sing to God, sing praises to His name; Lift up a song for Him who rides through the deserts, Whose name is the LORD, and exult before Him." And Psalm 50:23 (NIV) says, "He who sacrifices thank offerings honors me, and he prepares the way so that I may show him the salvation of God."

Meditate on the amazing story in 2 Chronicles 20. It's a striking example of what happens when God's people pray with a major emphasis on praise.

The chapter reports a dramatic battle with overwhelming odds against God's people. The main character, King Jehoshaphat, is terrified; so he gathers the people to pray. He begins with praise, extolling God as ruler over all the kingdoms of the earth, so powerful that no one could stand against Him; and he offers praise for past victories. Then he lays before the Lord his urgent problem: "We are powerless before this great multitude who are coming against us; nor do we know what to do, but our eyes are on Thee" (v. 12). The reply: "Do not fear or be dismayed...the battle is not yours but God's" (v. 15). And the response: worship and more praise. Notice how King Jehoshaphat sandwiched his simple request for help between two thick slices of praise and worship.

The next day the army went forth to face the enemy, believing and praising God. "And when they began singing and praising" (v. 22), the Lord set ambushes against the enemy forces, and they were totally destroyed. Not one soldier escaped alive.

The result of the battle? Great enrichment. It took three days to gather the treasures found in the enemy camp.

What were the keys that moved God's mighty hand? Much praise, a simple request, faith in God's Word, and then as a sign of that faith, worship and still more praise. As in an earlier battle during the reign of Jehoshaphat's grandfather, "The sons of Judah conquered because they trusted in the LORD" (2 Chronicles 13:18).

Praise can play a highly significant role in moving the mighty hand of God in your life, bringing not only deliverance but also enrichment for you and glory to His name.

THROUGH PRAISE YOU CAN PROFIT MORE FROM YOUR TRIALS

Why should you praise and give thanks in the midst of trials? Surely not because all the things that happen to you are in themselves good! The reason for praising in tough situations is found in Romans 8:28: "We know that God causes all things to work together for good to those who love God, to those who are called according to His purpose."

C. H. Welch has elaborated on this truth as follows:

> The Lord may not definitely have planned that this should overtake me, but He has most certainly permitted it. Therefore though it were an attack of an enemy, by the time it reaches me, it has the Lord's permission and therefore all is well. He will make it work together with all life's experiences for good.

Praise can heighten your awareness that distressing circumstances are God's blessings in disguise. Your trials rip away the flimsy fabric of your self-sufficiency. This makes room for God's Spirit to weave into your life a true and solid confidence—the kind of confidence that Paul expressed in Philippians 4:13: "I can do all things through Christ who strengthens me" (NKJV).

As fire melts unrefined silver, bringing the impurities to the surface, so trials bring the "scum" to the top in your life. When you praise God in the midst of a trial, you cooperate with His plan to remove the scum; when you complain, you resist His plan and stir the impurities right back into your character. This means that God, to accomplish His good purposes, may have to send or permit another trial; it may delay the unfolding of His good plan for you and your loved ones.

Through praise you focus your attention on God. You acknowledge Him as your source of overcoming power. You begin to look at your problems from a new perspective—you compare them with your mighty, unlimited God. You see them as molehills rather than mountains, as opportunities rather than hindrances, as stepping stones instead of stumbling blocks. You have a part in making them the prelude to new victories, the raw materials for God's miracles.

Praise helps you obey God's command in James 1:2–4 (Phillips), "When all kinds of trials and temptations crowd into your lives, my brothers, don't resent them as intruders, but welcome them as friends! Realize that they come to test your faith and to produce in you the quality of endurance." Praise is a catalyst that speeds up God's maturing process in your life.

PRAISE CAN HELP YOU EXPERIENCE CHRIST AS YOUR LIFE

In Colossians 3:4 we read, "Christ...is our life." I find this one of the most significant truths in the whole New Testament. The Lord began to open up its meaning to me years ago through a man of God who made the statement, "It's not only true that my life is Christ's, but my life is Christ." What an amazing truth! Christ is my life! And yours! Think of who Christ is and what He is like! Then think of what it means to have Him as your indwelling life— what it means in being obedient and loving, in being adequate, in being joyful. Again and again I find release and strength as I simply say, "Thank You, Father, that Christ is my life."

I find that praise is a tremendous aid in experiencing this truth. Praise stimulates my faith, helping me believe that something tremendous has taken place deep inside me—that God has infused me with the person and life of His Son. As I praise the Lord for who His Son is—pure and holy, loving and powerful—I can go on to praise Him that this is what He is in me.

God has used Romans 6 to greatly expand my experience of this life-changing truth, and year after year the Holy Spirit deepens my understanding of what Paul is saying. I'm still learning more, but I'd like to share with you how this chapter has helped me.

Do you find Romans 6 somewhat confusing? If so, you're not alone! So have I! And Warren tells me that he prayed off and on for nine years about what it meant before the Lord gave him his first delightful breakthrough in understanding this chapter. So I'm praying that the Holy Spirit will use the following paragraphs to give you glimpses into what Paul is saying—or for some of you, to deepen your already rich experience of its truths. It may not be the easiest reading. So before you begin, why not pray that the Holy Spirit will teach you?

Before we start, be aware that this chapter does not teach us that being "dead to sin" means that sin no longer affects us, that it no longer appeals to us. It does not tell us to envision ourselves as corpses that, when kicked or stomped upon, won't feel a thing, won't get mad, won't hit back. The chapter tells us that we're dead to sin, but in the next breath—in the same sentence—it tells us we're alive with the resurrected life of Christ.

We see this in verse 11: "Consider yourselves to be dead to sin, but alive to God in Christ Jesus."

Let's take a look at the context of this verse. Paul has been talking about the kind of persons we are, not through our natural birth but through our spiritual birth. When we were born of the Holy Spirit, we became one with Christ; we were united to Him.

What does this mean to us? It means that we became partakers of Christ's death and all its benefits; we were acquitted from all our guilt, for we "died to sin." We no longer live under the reign of sin.

But the miracle didn't stop there. Because Christ was raised to new life, we were raised with Him as new persons who had new life. God delivered us out of Satan's kingdom of sin and spiritual death, and He lifted us into Christ's kingdom—into the realm called "newness of life." Here in this kingdom we are alive with the very life of our risen Lord. And because we are alive with His life, we're righteous with His righteousness (2 Corinthians 5:21).

So we have ended our relationship with sin and guilt and death and have entered into an intimate, eternal relationship with God. We can relate to Him in a totally new way. We are dead to sin and alive to God.

But what does it mean to be dead to sin? Death never means being annihilated. It means being separated. So in our innermost being we have been separated from sin; sin is no longer our nature and we no longer need to let it be our master. According to Romans 7, sin still indwells us; the old sinful patterns and potential are still written in our minds and bodies. But we are to see ourselves in the light of the cross and the empty tomb. These stand within us as a powerful barrier between indwelling sinfulness and the new person we truly are in our innermost being. We're to let them serve as a powerful blockade, separating our new selves from what remains of our old sinful tendencies. The Cross and the empty tomb form an immovable boundary between who we were and who we have become, between our former realm of sin and guilt and death and our new realm of righteousness and life.

So we are dead to sin and alive to God. This is not fantasy. It is fact. It's the way things are in our genuine nature—in our innermost person, indwelt by the Holy Spirit, with Christ as our life.

It's not that sin no longer entices us. Sin fights against the Holy Spirit within us for control of our bodies and our personalities. And sin is cagey. It masquerades as our master who deserves our loyalty. It poses as an essential part of us, pretending to be our true nature, concerned about what is best for us. Then if we yield to its demands or swallow its bait, it either dulls our consciences or plagues us with guilt, whipping us even after we confess to the Lord. In countless ways indwelling sin causes us distress, struggles, and defeats.

But from God's viewpoint, it is not our true, new self who sins, but sin that still lives in us (Romans 7:17, 20). Our sins spring from our old sinful tendencies that are no longer our true identity. The real you, the real me, hates sin and is aligned against it. The real you is distressed when sin prevails and longs for your whole personality to be conformed to the image of Christ. The real you is dead to sin and alive to God.

Picture in your mind what will happen when you die physically. Your spirit, your personality, the new and true you, will immediately go to be with Christ (2 Corinthians 5:8). You will leave behind all your sinful tendencies, all your old patterns of living. And when Christ returns He will give you your new, imperishable, glorious, powerful, spiritual body, totally free of even the slightest remnant of sin and death (1 Corinthians 15:42–44).

Think of the freedom from sin's guilt and power you will then experience! Imagine the total way you will be dead to sin and alive to God! Then let the truth dawn on you: In your innermost being, as a "new creation" through Christ's life in you, this has already happened to you spiritually! This is not make-believe. God says it is true, so it is true.

God wants us to believe Him. He asks us to consider ourselves to be what we are: dead to sin but alive to God in Christ Jesus. He wants us to count on the fact that we have a new nature, a new identity. We're no longer to identify with our old identity, with our former nature, with who we once were, as though no radical change has taken place deep within us. As Christ is one with the Father in life and power, so we are one with Christ in life and power. Sin is no longer our nature; it is no longer our master. We are new persons, dead to sin and alive to God.

Think of it this way. It's as though in your innermost being you were previously a caterpillar; you entered the cocoon of Christ's death and through His resurrection emerged as a butterfly. Now, bit by bit as you follow Christ, the ways you think, feel, choose, and live are also being liberated and transformed. And you look forward to the day when your slowly dying body, with its weakness and sinful tendencies, will be changed into a glorious, radiant body just like our risen Lord's.

Thanking and praising God for these facts will help you see yourself as God sees you. This is vital, for we live as who we see ourselves to be. These truths don't just make you feel better about yourself. Rather, they lay the groundwork for a life of fuller obedience.

You can simply say, "Thank You, Lord, that I have been crucified with Christ. It is no longer I who live, but Christ is living in me. And the life that I now (this moment) live in my body, I live by faith in Your Son, who loved me, and sacrificed Himself for me (Galatians 2:20). I yield my entire body to You, as an instrument of righteousness, to do Your will. I praise You that Christ in me is infinitely greater than all the power of sin in me. Thank You that He has set me free from the condemnation of sin, and that His resurrected life is more powerful than the downward pull of sin!"

Praise the Lord often for the massive difference He has made in you through your new birth and the new, eternal, spiritual life that is yours in Christ. Such praise can help you view yourself as a new person, and therefore live the new life God has in mind for you.

The Holy Spirit wants to saturate our minds with the truths He has revealed in the Bible, including these truths in Romans 6. As we meditate on them and respond with praise for them, He delivers us from begging God for what He has already given us. He wants us to pray; prayer is basic to His working. But He wants us to pray with understanding and with praise.

How do we often pray? We plead for victory when Christ is in us as our more-than-conquering life. We beg for the Holy Spirit as though He were not already indwelling us, as though He were not yearning for our consent to fill and control us and produce His fruit in our lives. We pray for spiritual and emotional resources as though they were external bonuses. We forget that they are part of our birthright in Christ, for in Him God has blessed us with every possible spiritual blessing, with everything we need for life and godliness (Ephesians 1:3; 2 Peter 1:3). We cry to the Lord to give us things that we already have because He is in us. He says, "I am the bread of life, the water of life, the light of life; I am the way, I am the truth, I am the resurrection and the life—I am what you need" (John 6:35; 7:37; 8:12; 14:6; 11:25). He wants us to reply, "Thank You, Lord, You are! You are my sufficiency this moment, this hour, this day. I'm counting on Your life in me—Your love and patience, Your gentleness and guidance and power—to meet my needs and overflow to others."

When we praise with thanksgiving, we deepen our experience of Christ in us as our Source. He constantly fills us and replenishes our resources as we give ourselves in loving service to other people.

C. S. Lewis wrote that a car is made to run on

gas, and it won't run properly on anything else. Likewise, God made us to run on Himself. He is the fuel our spirits were designed to burn and the food our spirits were designed to feed on. So it's no use trying to find inner release and power and fulfillment apart from God. There is no such thing. And God has given us His life and power through our inner union with Christ Jesus our Lord.

As we turn our attention to Christ, focusing on Him and His sufficiency, how can we help but praise Him that He is our life?

Praise Can Help You Demonstrate God's Reality in a Secular, Materialistic Society

What are the prevailing views of our age? Many people view life through the lens of naturalism—the belief that all things can be explained by natural causes, and that if there is a supernatural realm, it has no effect on the natural world or on our day-by-day living.

A major offshoot of such thinking is secularism,

which is one of the most widely embraced views of life in our day. Secularism means that God and His will have no part in life. The only things that really matter are human and materialistic concerns. So the secular person, being indifferent to God or actually rejecting Him, lives only for this present world and its rewards.

As you praise and pray, you make your circumstances and your life a test tube that demonstrates the existence of a personal God, a God who is present and involved and who controls the natural universe. The fact that He intervenes and overrules in your daily situations and concerns becomes more clear to you. This flushes out false views of life that still cling to your thinking. It also makes God more obvious to people around you.

Praise (and we're talking about praise rooted in God's Word, praise bent on God's glory) can also help deliver you from secular values. It turns your attention to spiritual and eternal values; it directs you away from the pleasure and success mentality of our age, which resists all pain and discomfort and delay. And it keeps you from trying to make God answerable to you for what He does or permits.

Praise can free you from wasting your energies by speculating on just exactly how each circumstance in your life could be part of God's plan. Through praising and thanking God, you put your stamp of approval on His unseen purposes. You do this not because you can figure out the specific whys or hows, but because you trust His love and wisdom. You endorse Paul's words in Romans 11:33–34 (Phillips):

> Frankly, I stand amazed at the unfathomable complexity of God's wisdom and God's knowledge. How could man ever understand His reasons for action, or explain His methods of working?

Praise Can Help You Overcome Satan and His Crafty Strategies

Who would have imagined that modern men and women, even the highly educated, would revolt against the spiritual vacuum produced by modern philosophies, and in their revolt would turn to spiritism, to the occult, to Satan worship? Satan inspired these philosophies; then as people abandon them, he directs them into even greater spiritual bondage.

Most of us as real believers steer clear of such obvious cooperation with Satan. So what does he do? He seeks to get us preoccupied with him in ways that seem to be strategic to our spiritual warfare. He promotes an excessive interest in himself, in his evil assistants, and in just how he has them organized.

It is important to know our enemy. The Bible gives us vital data about Satan and his accomplices, and we can learn much from experienced spiritual warriors who base their warfare on the Scriptures. But Satan tries to sidetrack us. He seeks to get us enemy-centered rather than Christ-centered. He prods us to delve into intriguing details about him and his cohorts, details we don't need to know in overcoming him—details that are not revealed in the Bible and that may be mere speculations or even lies from evil spirits. In one way or another Satan tries to get us fascinated, or even obsessed, with himself, with demons, with demonization.

One pastor tells how he and his people got snared into giving demons undue prominence in their services. Demons, he said, began to flock to the meetings; demon after demon had to be cast out of people. After all, evil spirits are like their father, the devil. They are proud; they are flattered by lots of attention; they love the limelight. So this pastor and his people backed off from focusing on demons and majored on praise that lifted the Lord high. And they found that most of their trouble with demonization disappeared.

As someone has put it, "It's a serious mistake to underestimate the power of Satan; it's a tragedy to overestimate it"—or to be overly occupied with it.

As demon influence and oppression increase, so does the urgency of focusing our attention on Jesus as Victor. Jesus came into Satan's territory and won the victory over Satan at every point of contest, both in His own life and in delivering people from demons. Finally, by means of the cross, He stripped the demonic authorities of their powers; He exposed them to be empty and defeated as He triumphed over them (Colossians 2:15). Then through the resurrection God demonstrated His incomparable, all-prevailing power—power that is now in us and available to us: "He raised him from the dead and gave him the place of supreme honor in heaven—a place that is infinitely superior to any conceivable command, authority, power or control, and which carries with it a name far beyond any name that could ever be used in this world or the world to come" (Ephesians 1:20–21, Phillips). God has placed all things under the feet of our Lord Jesus Christ—and that includes Satan and every one of the evil beings associated with him.

How does this relate to praise? Praise is a powerful weapon against Satan. Satan hates praise. It reminds him that God is still supreme in spite of all his evil efforts throughout all the ages. It rubs in the fact of his inferiority, his limitations.

Any praise thwarts Satan. But to make your praise even more powerful against him, couple it with God's Word, and especially with truths that magnify Jesus as Victor. Include praise for the blood of Christ, the victory won on the cross, and the triumph of the Resurrection. Extol your risen Lord and His exalted position. Lift up His name in triumphant faith. Such praise is powerful in defeating Satan and his clever deceptions.

We may or may not know the names of our demonic opponents, or their rank; we may or may not be well-versed in occultic practices or in New Age tactics or in just what satanists are up to. But through praise we can defeat our enemy; we can thwart his purposes and advance the purposes of our wonderful Lord.

Some years ago I was helping a young woman named Betty, who had grown up in a family that worshiped idols and constantly sought to appease evil spirits. Every time she went home, she felt intense demonic oppression. So we studied the Word of God about Satan and his ways. But far more, we studied about our Victor and how to overcome the enemy through the Word, through prayer and praise, through putting on the armor of God. The next time Betty returned home, she fortified herself with the truths she had learned—as well as praise for the Lord Jesus Christ, for His triumph over Satan and all his hordes of evil helpers, and for His victorious power. And God protected her from even the slightest demonic oppression. She returned radiant and rejoicing.

We can apply Psalm 149:6 to our spiritual warfare, as we rejoice in God's triumph over the enemy: "Let the high praises of God be in their mouth, and a two-edged sword in their hand."

THROUGH PRAISE YOU CAN BRING GLORY AND PLEASURE TO GOD

Through praise you give God something no one else in heaven or earth can give: the love and adoration of your heart. He chose you before He created the earth; He designed you as a unique original, so that you would be a special person unlike any other; He made you for Himself. And He has made plans for an intimate relationship with you throughout all eternity. Such a God is not indifferent to your response to Him. Your praise makes Him glad. Your neglect grieves Him.

Did you know that praise can help you fulfill your destiny, your chief purpose in this life and the next? The Westminster Catechism condenses volumes of scriptural truth when it says:

> The chief end of man is to glorify God
> and to enjoy Him forever.

Through worship, praise, and thanksgiving you minister directly to God, who seeks for people to worship Him. Here lies the most compelling reason for praise.

God does not enjoy your praise because He's conceited and loves the limelight. He enjoys it because praise is an indispensable part of relating to Him, the Creator and Supreme Ruler who is exalted high above all. God is holy and infinite and all powerful, and you and I are specks in a vast universe, who receive from Him life and breath and all things. So worship, praise, and thanksgiving bring needed realism into our fellowship with Him. They make possible a true, deep, mutually satisfying relationship.

But does God delight in all praise?

Sometimes people try to attach praise onto an indifferent or self-willed life, hoping for an emotional lift or special visible rewards. And sometimes even a disobedient Christian can get into the mood of group worship or experience a high while listening to praise cassettes. After all, pagans worshiping false gods can experience times of ecstasy! But neither the disobedient Christian nor the pagan honors the true and living God. So how can their praise be a joy to God?

Worship is more than an emotional turn-on. Worship includes offering ourselves to God, to be His servants and to do His will—nothing more, nothing less, nothing else. It means that we radically change our goals. We choose basic life goals that are centered in God: to know Him better, to love Him with all our being, to do His will at any cost, to glorify Him, and to please Him.

A friend of mine, who serves Christ as a professional in a restricted country, came across a quote from Amy Carmichael that says, "O Lord Jesus, my Beloved, may I be a joy to Thee." She has made this her major and constant prayer request. Above her desire for marriage (she's single and not too young), above her desire for success, above her desire to see friends and loved ones half a world away, she has chosen this supreme desire, "May I be a joy to Thee." That's worship.

In worship you bow humbly before the Lord, yielding to Him as fully as you know how at this point in your life. Out of such surrender and worship flows the kind of praise that fully honors and glorifies and delights God. Out of them flow not only your set times of praise, but also, as the hours roll by, moments of spontaneous praise, silent or spoken as the situation requires. You think of who God is or of something He has done. Then your heart overflows with adoration or gratefulness as Paul's did in 1 Timothy 1:17, when he broke into his train of thought with the words, "Now to the King eternal, immortal, invisible, the only God, be honor and glory forever and ever. Amen."

Or you thank and praise Him although your feelings resist rather than assist you. It's all right if your praise comes out of a life that has struggles, a life that still falls short of the glory of God, a life that has defeats that require confession, and a life that slides into emotional low periods. This is part of being human in a fallen world, waiting for the magnificent future God has planned for us—for life on a new earth, in a body glorious beyond our wildest imaginings.

It may be that often your praise is joyful and enthusiastic. But God doesn't enjoy your praise on the basis of how warm and happy you're feeling. As C. S. Lewis said, we may honor God more in our low times than in our peak times. You may bring Him special joy when you find yourself depressed or wiped out emotionally—when you look around at a world from which God seems to have vanished, and you choose to trust Him and praise Him in spite of how you feel.

Your worship and praise enriches all that God wants to do through your life. A. W. Tozer wrote,

> We're here to be worshipers first and workers only second.... The work done by a worshiper will have eternity in it.*

As you fill your life with praise, God will reveal Himself to you in new ways—and not only to you but also through you to other people. More and more, in every situation, you'll shed abroad His fragrance.

What is our chief goal? "To glorify God and to enjoy Him forever" (Westminster Catechism). This is our high calling, our destiny. And praise is one of the greatest, most important ways to fulfil it.

* A. W. Tozer, *Gems from Tozer* (Send the Light Trust, 1969), 7.

ACTS OF PRAISE

YOUR MOST BASIC ACT OF WORSHIP

Lord, I'm Yours. Whatever the cost may be, may Your will be done in my life. I realize I'm not here on earth to do my own thing, or to seek my own fulfillment or my own glory. I'm not here to indulge my desires, to increase my possessions, to impress people, to be popular, to prove I'm somebody important, or to promote myself. I'm not here even to be relevant or successful by human standards. I'm here to please You.

I offer myself to You, for You are worthy. All that I am or hope to be, I owe to You. I'm Yours by creation, and every day I receive from You life and breath and all things. And I'm Yours because You bought me, and the price You paid was the precious blood of Christ. You alone, the Triune God, are worthy to be my Lord and Master. I yield to You, my gracious and glorious heavenly Father; to the Lord Jesus who loved me and gave Himself for me; to the Holy Spirit and His gracious influence and empowering.

All that I am and all that I have I give to You.

I give You any rebellion in me, which resists doing Your will. I give You my pride and self-dependence, which tell me I can do Your will in my own power if I try hard enough. I give You my fears, which tell me I'll never be able to do Your will in some areas of life. I consent to let You energize me...to create within me, moment by moment, both the desire and the power to do Your will.

I give You my body and each of its members...my entire inner being: my mind, my emotional life, my will...my loved ones...my marriage or my hopes for marriage...my abilities and gifts...my strengths and weaknesses...my health...my status (high or low)...my possessions...my past, my present, and my future...when and how I'll go Home.

I'm here to love You, to obey You, to glorify You. O my Beloved, may I be a joy to You!

Aren't You Grateful?

Aren't you grateful for the delight and privilege of praising our wonderful God, the most beautiful and generous and trustworthy of all beings!

As you go through these thirty-one days of praise month by month, you will enjoy more fully the vast wonder of who God is. He in turn will enrich and refresh you and find special joy in you.

As the Lord directs your heart to further aspects of who He is and what He does, you may also want to begin creating additional paragraphs of praise. You can glean ideas from the Scriptures and from other sources, such as sermons, songs, quotations, and poems.

> By him therefore let us offer the sacrifice
> of praise to God continually, that is, the
> fruit of our lips giving thanks to his name.
> (Hebrews 13:15, KJV)

An Invitation to Continue

You have now completed your first thirty-one-day journey of praise. Why not celebrate how much this has meant to God by reviewing "Through Praise You Can Bring Glory and Pleasure to God," page 143. Isn't this a great motivation to keep on praising—to begin another thirty-one-day journey?

Many people travel through the "31 Days of Praise" in part 2 month after month and find that the trip gets better each time they make it.

I invite you to join them.

The publisher and author would love to hear your comments about this book. *Please contact us at:*
www.multnomah.net/31days

OTHER BOOKS AND BIBLE STUDIES BY WARREN AND RUTH MYERS

Praise: A Door to God's Presence will further enrich your understanding of praise and your enjoyment of God.*

Pray: How to Be Effective in Prayer will help you maintain an exciting, growing prayer life.*

The Quiet Time is a booklet that motivates and gives practical help for the quiet time.

*These books available only from:

Castle Bookstore
PO Box 6000
Colorado Springs, Colorado 80934
719-272-7410
OR

The Navigators, Singapore

117 Lorong K

Telok Kurau

425758

fax 65/344-0975

e-mail navsing@singnet.com.sg.

*Experiencing God's Attributes**

*Experiencing God's Presence**

Discovering God's Will
(ISBN: 1-57683-178-7)

These three Bible study books have helped
thousands discover rich truths about God and learn
how to experience Him in their hearts and lives.
They are excellent for personal study and group
discussion.

Except as indicated, these books are available
from your local bookstore or Castle Bookstore.

*These books are presently out of print, but you
can order attractive photocopies from Castle
Bookstore.

How Do I Pray?

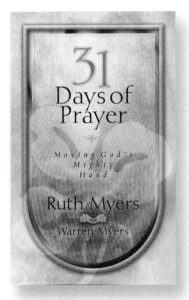

31 Days of Prayer:
Moving God's Mighty Hand

It takes but a few weeks to form a habit. Readers of the re-release of *31 Days of Prayer* can form a prayer habit that lasts a lifetime with this beautiful and practical devotional. Authors Ruth and Warren Myers show readers how to grow in prayer, even if the amount of time set aside seems small at first. The book guides believers through prayer for thirty-one days, allowing for personalized prayer that reflects individual circumstances and needs for spiritual growth. *31 Days of Prayer* leads readers step-by-step into praying about what is close to their hearts and God's.

ISBN 1-57673-874-4

31 Days of Prayer Journal

Use of this beautiful and practical version of *31 Days of Prayer*, which includes space for journaling, can form a prayer habit that lasts a lifetime.

ISBN 1-57673-099-9

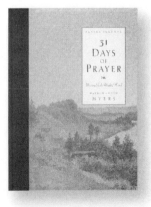